An Analysis
of
Dream in Indian Philosophy

Sri Garib Dass Oriental Series No. 99

AN ANALYSIS OF DREAM IN INDIAN PHILOSOPHY

SATYAJIT LAYEK

SRI SATGURU PUBLICATIONS
A Division of
Indian Books Centre
Delhi, India.

Published by:

Sri Satguru Publications,
Indological & Oriental Publishers,
A Division of
Indian Books Centre,
40/5, Shakti Nagar,
Delhi - 10007
INDIA.

First Edition:- Delhi 1990.

ISBN-81-7030-225-0

Printed in India.

DEDICATED
to the
LOTUS FEET
of
Prof. R. Mukherjee
Ex-Vice-Chancellor,
Rabindrabharati University,
Calcutta.

TABLE OF CONTENTS

FOREWORD

The present work is the thesis of Dr. Satyajit Layek which was accepted by the Poona University for the degree of Ph.D. The work was completed under my supervision. I am happy to see that it is being printed now.

In search of Truth, the Indian Philosophical systems have given a lot of thinking to the age-old question of Reality. Almost every system has to say something about it. Nobody denied the fact that one's behaviour depends upon clear knowledge of things, technically called *savikalpaka-jñāna.* Nobody could also deny that we come to know the existence of a thing through this knowledge *(jñānādhīnā vastusattā).* But they differed in holding the views whether the things shown by a clear knowledge are real or not. Neither the realists nor the idealists held different opinions regarding cognitions having objects.

Everything in the world of ours is momentary and thereby everything results into pain *(sarbam duḥkham).* There is nothing called permanent pleasure, according to them.

As against this the Advaitins held the view that although it is a fact that everything in this world is momentary, still there is something called the highest Truth or Brahman or Bliss which is permanent. Thus, they felt the necessity to establish three kinds of realities called *Vyāvahārika-sattā, Prātibhāsika-sattā,* and *Pāramarthika-sattā.* As long as we are behaving with things we are required to accept those things as real; these things are said to have *vyāvahārika-sattā.* The *prātibhāsika-sattā* exists in a thing which has existence during the duration of its cognition alone. And the ultimate reality is the *pāramārthika-sattā,* but when I see silver on a conch-shell, it has existence only for the duration of the cognition of the silver after seeing a conch-shell and thus it has *prātibhāsika-sattā* or *jñ*ānaika-sattā. That which is true for past, present and future is the ultimate Truth and that has *pāramārthika-sattā.*

Śrīharṣa, in his *Khaṇḍanakhaṇḍa-khādya,* observes that the difference between the silver in the shop and that seen in the conch-shell is of the duration of time only. The silver did exist for the seer of the conch-cell till he came to know that it is not silver, but a conch-shell. Similarly, the silver in the shop is also going to loose its existence or reality after it is known that it is not silver after the realisation of the ultimate reality, the Brahman.

The point is made more clear by bringing the case of the seeing of silver which exists till the dreaming of the silver and it looses its existence after it is known that it is not a real silver, but merely a dream-silver.

Thus, the difference of the silver after seeing the conch-shell, the silver in the dream is also of merely duration of time. While the conch-shell-silver exists till one approaches it and finds that it is not a silver, the dream-silver exists only, during the dreaming of the silver. Śrīharṣa holds that in the same manner what we consider now to be real silver in the shop is also going to be contradicted after the Brahman is known. Thus, it is only the duration of time that varies. What we consider to be real silver is not different from the dream-silver in reality. The difference is only in the duration of time.

These philosophers made use of the simile of dream-object in order to deny the utlimate reality of this world of ours with which we behave consistently.

Dr. Satyajit Layek has analysed this phenomenon of dreaming from the point of view of Indian Philosophy as well as from the point of view of western Psychology. The physiology of dream is also described and at the same time the use of the simile of dream is also properly analysed. The epistemology of a dream-cognition has also been attempted here. Finally, all these findings after the analysis of Indian view-points are compared with the findings of western Psychology and Medical Science.

The present work may be considered as a good specimen of analytic inter-disciplinary approach to the study of Indian Philosophy and modern Psychology. A dream is analysed from all angles and its use for solving philosophical issues has been projected in right perspective.

I am confident that scholars and students of Indian Philosophy and Psychology will welcome this work of Dr. Layek and thereby will encourage the author to take up research work with more and more seriousness.

V. N. Jha.

Poona
23.6.89

ACKNOWLEDGEMENTS

At the very outset, it is my paramount duty to convey sincere sense of indebtedness to my revered Guru Prof. V.N. Jha, Director of the centre of Advanced Study in Sanskrit, who initiated me into the field of Indian Philosophy.

I express my unfathomable sense of gratitude to the Patron of Sanskrit learners Prof. R. Mukherjee, Ex-Vice-Chancellor, Rabindrabharati University, Calcutta, because of whose benign grace I could pursue my research study.

I am very much grateful to Prof. S.D. Joshi, Ex-Director of this Centre, who extended all the necessary facilities during my stay in Poona.

It is indeed difficult to express my deep sense of respect through language to my parents, Brother, Brother-in-law, sister, sister-in-law and Father-in-law for their affection, invaluable blessings, moral advice and encouragement which enabled me to come up to this level.

My choicest blessings are also due for our little 'BAPI', whose unintelligible speech inspired to accelerate my work for meeting her at my earliest. My best regards are for Pt. T.S. Śrinivāsa Śāstri, who enlightened and introduced me in the field of Buddhist Logic. I owe a lot to Dr. Goswami, Dr. Bhavasar and Dr. Saha for familiarizing me with advanced materials.

I shall be failing in my duty if I don't acknowledge the help extended by Dr. C.G. Despande, a Psycho-analyst and Prof. V. Sukla for their instruction to find out solution of the intricate problems.

I must keep on record the help and ready co-operation rendered by the staff of C.A.S.S. Library, Jayakar Library, B.O.R.I. Library and Deccan College Library.

Finally, I thank Mr. Naresh Gupta & Sunil Gupta of M/s Indian Books Centre, for bringing out this book in such a short span of time.

Calcutta
Rakṣābandhanam
The 16th Aug. '89

Satyajit Layek

LIST OF ABBREVIATIONS

Abhi.Ko.bhā	Abhidharmakoṣabhāṣya
ABORI	Annals of Bhandarkar Oriental Research Institute.
Adv. Saṁ.	Advayavajrasaṁgraha.
Ag. Brā.	Agnyādheya Brāhmaṇa
Ait.Ār.	Aitareya Āraṇyaka
Ait. Upa.	Aitareyopaniṣad.
Ālam. Parī.	Ālambanaparīkṣā
Aṇu. bhā.	Aṇubhāṣya
Aru. Ahṛśa.	Aruṇatīkā on Aṣtāṅgahṛdayaśarīram.
Asaṁsū.	Aṣṭāṅgasaṁgrahasūtram
Bhā.	Bhāṣya
Bhā. bhā.	Bhāskarabhāṣya
Bhām	Bhāmatī
Bodhi. Pañjikā	Bodhicāryāvatāra Pañjikā
Bṛ.	Bṛhati
Brā.	Brāhmaṇa
Bṛ.Upa.	Bṛhadāraṇyakopaniṣad
B.S.Ś.	Brahmasūtra Śaṅkarabhāṣya
B.Ss.	Brahmasūtras
Ca. Ind.	Caraka Indriyasthānam
Ca. Saṁ.	Carakasaṁhitā.
Chā. Upa	Chāndogyopaniṣad
Gau. Bhā	Gauḍapāda Bhāṣya
Germ.	German
Gk.	Greek
Gopa. Brā	Gopatha Brāhmaṇa
Jai. Brā	Jaiminīya Brahmaṇa
Jai. Saṁ	Jaiminīya Saṁhitā
Jaya	Jayamaṅgalā
Kaṭha. Upa.	Kaṭhopaniṣad
Kāṭha. Saṁ.	Kāṭhaka Saṁhitā
Kau. Saṁ.	Kauthuma Saṁhitā

Kir.	Kiraṇāvalī
Ku. Brā	Kuṣmāṇḍa Brāhmaṇa
Lat.	Latin
Mā. bhā	Mādhvabhāṣya
Mā. Kā	Māṇḍukyakārikā
Mad.kā.	Mādhyandina Saṁhitā
Mā. Saṁ.	Madhyamakakārikā (i.e. Madhyamakaśāstra)
Mahā. Upa.	Mahopaniṣad
Mai. Upa	Maitrāyaṇyupaniṣad
Māṇḍū.Upa	Māṇḍūkyopaniṣad
ME	Middle English
NBh.	Nyāyabhāṣya
NV	Nyāyavārtika
NVT	Nyāyavārtikatātparyatīkā
Nyā. Kan	Nyāya Kandalī
Nyā.Ko.	Nyāya Koṣa
Nyā. ku.	Nyāya kusumāñjali
Nyā. Lī	Nyāyalīlāvatī
Nyā. Mañ.	Nyāyamañjarī
Nyā.Muktā.	Nyāyamuktāvali
Nyā.Pañ	Nyāvapadapañcikā
Nyā.pra. Vṛ	Nyāyapraveśavṛtti
Nyā.sā	Nyāyasāra
Nyā.sū	Nyāyasūtra
OE.	Old English
Paip. Saṁ.	Paipallāda Saṁhitā
PIE	Proto-Indo-European
Pra. Vā.	Pramāṇavārtika
Praśasta.bhā	Praśastapādabhāṣya
Praśna. Upa	Praśnopaniṣad
Prat.Khan.	Pratyakṣakhaṇḍa
Rā.Bā.	Rāmāyaṇa Bālakāṇḍa
Ṛv. Saṁ	Ṛgveda Saṁhitā
Śāb. bhā.	Śābarabhāṣya
Sāṁ. Sū	Sāṁkhyasūtra
Śāṅ. Ār.	Śāṅkhyāyana-Āraṇyaka
Śaṅ. Bhā.	Śaṅkarabhāṣya

Sap. Padā	Saptapadārthī
Śārī.Upa	Śārīrakopaniṣad
Ṣarva. D. Saṁ	Sarvadarśanasaṁgraha
Sarva M. Saṁ	Sarvamatasaṁgraha
Śat. Brā.	Śatapatha Brāhmaṇa
Śau. Saṁ	Śauṇaka Saṁhitā
Sid. Can.	Siddhānta Candrodaya
Sing.	Singular.
Skt.	Sanskrit
Śrī. bhā.	Śribhāṣya
Śrimad. Gītā	Śrimadbhagavadgītā.
Sū.	Sūtra.
Sū. Śarī	Suśrutaśarīram.
Svetā. Upa.	Svetāśvatar Upaniṣad
T.C.	Tattvacintāmaṇi
T. Vai.	Tattva Vaiśāradī
Tai. Brā	Taittirīya Brāhmaṇa
Tai. Upa	Taittirīyopaniṣad
Tar. bhā.	Tarkabhāṣā
Tarkā	Tarkāmṛta
Tar. Saṁ	Tarkasaṁgraha
Tat. Saṁ	Tattvasaṁgraha
Upa.	Upaskāra
Upā. Brā	Upānayana Brāhmaṇa
Upas.	Upaniṣads
V. Bhā.	Vyāsa Bhāṣya
Vai. Sū.	Vaiśeṣikasūtra
Vai.Sū. Vivṛ	Vaiśeṣikasūtravivṛti.
Vār.	Vārtika
Vṛ	Vṛtti
Yo. Ko.	Yoga. Koṣa
Yoga. Upa.	Yogaśikhopaniṣad
Yuk.	Yuktidīpikā

CHAPTER 1
INTRODUCTION

1.0. BACKGROUND

Interest in dream can be traced from the dawn of the human race. At the same time, it has been the human nature to enquire about its reality. More or less, it is an agreed fact that the dream-phenomenon is unreal. Nevertheless, it is a super-sensuous activity of the mind. So it is extremely difficult to analyse this type of mental activity in a concrete form. As we know, Philosophy remains in search of reality. Thus, a philosophical approach to the study of dream was a long-felt desideratum. Moreover, the study of dream-phenomenon has not been carried out from this perspective, in the light of Western Psychological and Philosophical findings.

Aristotle was the first Philosopher in the west to point out dream as a free psychic phenomenon. After that many works have been done on this discipline of study. Freud, Adler and Jung have tried their best to putforth their views. In the Orient, Praśastapāda, the commentator of Kaṇāda sūtras echoed the same view. Although, Philosophical literatures have recorded the analysis of dream, there has been no attempt to systematically arrange them and analyse them at one place. The present work is an interdisciplinary type of work. The main aim and object of this study is to compare and contrast the analysis of various dream phenomena of Indian Philosophies with that of the western tradition.

Vedānta and Jaina Philosophies hold the view that dreams are god-sent and a person gets dream due to his merit and demerit acquired by activities during his life time. In other words, in a way, it is not at all a mental creation. The later commentators kept on commenting without any change of the thesis. In short, without deviating from their standpoint they thought to follow their earlier

Philosophy without examining arguments critically.

On the otherhand, Nyāya-Vaiśeṣika, Sāṁkhya-Yoga, Mīmāṁsā etc. are of the opinion that dream is produced by *saṁskāra* and since it is produced by *saṁskāra* it is on par with *smṛti*. Because, *smṛti* also is caused by *saṁskāra*.

The analysis of dream appears in the context of determining reality of the world. It has been observed that there has been a common trend to cite dream--knowledge in order to demonstrate that the world is an illusion. This was first cited in the *Upaniṣadic* literature. After that it has been universalized. Whenever we find a clash between idealists and the realists for the acceptance or non-acceptance of the external objective reality, with which we are concerned in day-to-day life the example of dream is provided. But as a matter of fact, if we accept the four states of consciousness viz. *Jāgrat, Svapna, Suṣupti* and *Turīya*, it would become obvious that one state differs from the other. So it is not logical to cite an instance from other state in order to support the fact of another state. Moreover, the present work examines the grounds to ascertain dream-knowledge as unreal of both the idealists and the realists.

A dream is produced and it is known. This fact can also be corroborated by our direct experience. But how it is produced and how it is known become a matter of investigation. An attempt is made in this direction also in the background of eastern and western findings. In other words, it is attempted to present the ontological, epistemological and Philosophical positions of a dream-knowledge and its content. Western Philosophers regard dream-knowledge as an unreal mental vision. On the contrary, Psychology gives much importance to the dream-phenomenon. According to them dream is not unreal, each and every element of dream is meaningful. Because, sometimes on the basis of dream they diagnose and prescribe medicine. We find in the Indian tradition also similar approach.

The range of the present study includes Vedic literature and eight main branches of Indian Philosophies viz. Nyāya-Vaiśeśika, Sāṁkhya-Yoga, Mīmāṁsā-Vedānta, Jainism and Buddhism.

While handling the vedic literature it has been pointed out how the radical meaning of the word *svapna* (i.e. sleep) developed from sleep to deep-sleep; deep-sleep to dream and at the later *saṁhitās* from dream to a deity.

About its anatomy and physiology and of its materials and sources, Psychologists have discussed elaborately. A parallel discussion occurs in the *Āyurveda* (i.e. the science of Indian medicine). It has contributed significantly in this context. Therefore, we have freely drawn from original sources as far as possible.

The present study is divided into two parts. Part I and Part II. Part one contains the Indian findings, and the second part presents the Western findings.

I.1 WHAT IS DREAM?

Every human being passes through two distinct stages: (i) awakened-state and (ii) sleeping state. In the first stage all the six sense organs work with their optimum efficiency and in the other state all of them stop functioning excepting the internal sense-organ namely, mind. In the sleeping-state mind alone works with the data already available inside in the form of *saṁskāras* and that time we have some sort of knowledge which is otherwise known as dream. So dream is a phenomenon which takes place during sleep. Both, Indian and western philosophers agree on this point.

Many Philosophers have tried to define what exactly the dream means. The first definition-cum-etymology of *svapna* (i.e. dream) is found in the Śat. Brā. It says "...svā apiyanti tasmāt svāpyayah. Svāpyayaḥ ha vai tam svapna iti ācakṣate....(10.5.2.14)".* *Śat. Brā.* derives this word as sva+api$\sqrt{}$i-to keep with in, take possession of, nestle. In the context of some mystical significance this word is used.1

The *Chā. Upa.* 6.8.1 says "Svapiti nāma....svam apito bhavati, tasmād enam svapiti iti ācakṣate, svam hi apito bhavati".* It is a kind of folk etymology. The word has been artificially split as 'sva apito bhavati'. The actual etymology of *svapna* will be from the √svap, but the *Śat. Brā* does not derive the word from it.2

Prof. Fatah Sing arrived at two meanings of the word *svapna* The first one is 'sleep' or 'dream' from the ∫suap and the second one is *prāṇa* from the ∫sva-ap.3

The *Saptapadārthī (Sap. Padā)* defines dream as "mental cognition when mind is vitiated by sleep."4

The *Siddhāntacandrodaya (Sid. Can)* defines *Svapna* as mental perversion[5]. The *Nyāyalīlāvati (Nyā. Lī.)* defines it as a knowledge which is produced because of the predominance of sleep.6 According to the western Psychologists dream is a free psychic phenomenon during sleep.*

So from the above discussion it can be summed up that Indian and Western traditions have agreed upon two points viz. dream is a mental phenomenon and it takes place during sleep. There is not much difference between these two traditions in defining dream. But David B. Klein while defining dream states that dream is a state of consciousness taking place during sleep. Further, he adds another clause to his statement that 'sleep' (in the conventional sense of the term) is not invariably necessary for the production of dream-consciousness and we cannot say that any state of awareness during sleep is dream[7]. We would like to draw readers' attention to a comparable Āyurvedic observation namely, a dream is the half-sleep and the half-awakened state of a dreamer.

I.2. WHAT IS A DREAM-KNOWLEDGE?

Knowledge is classified into two categories, ***anubhava*** (the direct perception) and *smaraṇa* (remembrance). ***Saṁskāras*** are left behind by our day-to-day experience. ***Smṛti*** is caused by the ***saṁskā ras***. Apart from *smṛti* all knowledges are included in ***anubhava***[8].

Anubhava is of two types: *Pramā* (i.e. the valid cognition) and *apramā* (invalid cognition). *Pramā* is of four sorts namely, *Pratyakṣa* (perception), *Anumāna* (inferencial cognition), *Upamā na* (analogical cognition) and *Śābda* (verbal cognition)[9].

According to Praśastapāda and Jagadīśa *apramā* is divided into four categories viz. *saṁśaya* (doubtful cognition), *viparyaya* (wrong-knowledge), *svapna* (dream knowledge) and *anadhyavasā ya* (indeterminate knowledge)[10].

Out of the four types of *apramā* Naiyāyikas include *svapna* and *anadyavasāya in viparyaya.* So we find only two divisions of *apramā* namely, *saṁśaya* and *viparyaya*'[11]. There has been a tendency among of the Indian Philosophers to classify this knowledge in either of these two groups viz. direct-perception or indirect-perception. Some of them designate themselves as the follower of presentative theory of knowledge (i.e. *anubhava* or direct perception). And those who follow the second theory label themselves as the follower of the representative theory of knowledge (i.e. *smarana* or indirect perception).

But as a matter of fact, dream-knowledge can no longer be designated as external *anubhava* (i.e. the direct perception). Because, it does not satisfy the stipulated criterion (i.e. the *indriyārtha sannikarṣa)* for net experience. Further, the answer may be given in the same way to the follower of the representative theory. Though both the knowledges do not require the existence of any object for their origination and both are caused by *saṁskāra* still, one knowledge (i.e. the dream-knowledge) cannot be equated with the other (i.e. the remembrance). Simply because, the very nature of remembrance is true and it can be verified with the external reality namely, the object of that remembrance.

Whereas dream-knowledge is unreal since it does not have correspondence with the external reality. Again, another difference can be made by saying that the remembrance is sometimes an effect of an endeavour but dream is an automatic flow. So both can never be one and the same. Very minute observation points out that if the cause for both knowledges is one and the same then how can we say in one case it will be real and in other one it will be unreal. So here we may deduce that if a dream-knowledge is caused by false impression then it will produce false-knowledge. On the contrary, if it is true-impression which produces dream-knowledge then the dream-knowledge has to be true. And hence, dream-knowledge can be classified either as false-remembrance or true-remembrance.

Indian and Western Philosophers as well as Psychologists are mainly concerned about its nature study. There too we find that they divide this knowledge into two groups-real and unreal. e.g. When Freud regards dream-knowledge as real, the other psychologist David B. Klein holds that it is a hallucinatory experience since it shows discrepancy with the external reality. The same view is also held by the Philosophers of both sides. Again, he points out that the unreality of dream-events may also be suggested by the derivation of the word dream, which is traced through the Anglo-Saxon to the root meaning of the modern German word 'traum', which in turn is related to the German verb 'trügen', which means 'to deceive'.

In the knowledge of dream *ātman* (the puruṣa) will be the *samavāyikāraṇa* (i.e. the material cause) and the *dhātu doṣas etc. (i.e. the defect of bodily humours) will be the nimittakāraṇa* (instrumental cause).

NOTES & REFERENCES

*[When he (the man in the eye) sleeps (svapiti) then vital airs] take possession of him as his own (svāpiyanti) and hence the term 'svāpyaya' (being taken possession of by one's own people) doubtless being mystically call 'svapna' (sleep). (Extract from the translation of Julius Eggeling).

1. *Etymology In The Brāhmaṇas,* pp, 395

*[Uddālaka says to śvetaketu (about the true nature of sleep) when a person enters into deep-sleep-state then he becomes united with Pure Being (Sat)]. This person goes to his own (self). This is why he is in deep sleep (svapiti), it is because he goes (apita) to his own (svam).

(Extract from the Translation of Swami Nikhilananda).

2. *Etymology In The Brahmaṇas*, pp. 395
3. *The Vedic Etymology*, pp. 233
4. *Nidrāduṣṭāntaḥkaraṇajam jñānam* svapnaḥ (Sap. Padā. pp. 125)
5. *Svapnomānasaviparyaya (Sid. can.* pp. 39)
6. *Nidrābhibḥūtajñanam* svapnaḥ(Nyā. Lī. pp. 765)

* It seems that Oxford Dictionary has summarized the definition of the western philosophers like Plato, Aristotle etc. It views that "A train of thoughts, images, or fancies passing through the mind during sleep; a vision during sleep." *(The Shorter Oxford Dictionary*, Vol. 1. p. 562)

7. *Encyclopedia Britannica*, Vol. 7. pp. 664
8 ....*Sā dividhā smṛti anubhavaśca. Saṁskāram janyam jñā* nam smṛtiḥ. Tadbinnam jñānam anubhavaḥ(Tar. Sam. pp. 21-22).
9. *Anubhavo dvividhaḥPramā 'yathārthaśca. Tatra pramā catur-vidhaḥ..* (Tarkā. pp. 46).
10. *Tatra avidyā caturvidhā saṁśaya-viparyaya-anadhyavasāya-svapnalakṣaṇā. (Praśasta. bhā. pp. 411). Ayathārthajñānam-* caturvidhah-saṁśaya-viparyayaḥ svapno'nadhyavasāyaśceti (Tarkā. pp. 46).
11. *Tatra Naiyāyikamate svapnādhyavasāyau viparyaya-madhye praviṣṭau. (Ibid. pp. 46)*

CHAPTER-II
INDIAN TRADITION
DREAM IN VEDIC LITERATURE

II.0 DREAM IN VEDIC LITERATURE

In the *Ṛgveda Saṁhitā (ṚV. Sam)* (1400 B.C.)* and in the other *saṁhitās* the word *svapna* occurs forty times as nominative singular, ten times as accusative sign., six times as instrumental sing, nine times as dative sing., once as genitive sing., thirteen times as locative sing. and once as locative plural. In total it occurs eighty times.

In the *Brāhmaṇas* (1000 B.C.) the word *svapna* occurs six times as nominative sing., six times as accusative sing., twice as instrumental sing., once as dative sing., once as ablative sing. and twice as locative sing; in total eighteen times.

The Indo-European synonyms of the skt. word *svapna* are as follows: Gk. en-ýpnion, Lat. Somnium, Italian, Sogno. OE. Swefn, Germ. Schlaf, ME. Sweven.[1]

In PIE language Swep (full grade or accented) is similar to Skt. Svap. (Non-accented or zero grade)[2]. The study of the word *svapna* reveals that in the *Saṁhitās* this word is used in various senses and these meanings can be related historically and logically.

It can be noticed that in the *Saṁhitās* the word *svapna* occurs in the following four senses:

(i) Sleep (ii) Prolonged sleep or Profound sleep
(iii) Dream and (iv) Dream as a deity. Let us see one by one:

(i) *Svapna in the sense of 'Sleep'.*

In the *Ṛv. Saṁ.* 8.2.18 we find that the seer is praying to the god Indra to keep the sacrificer away from *svapna*[3].

The conventional meaning of *Svapna* is dream. The word *Svapna* is interpreted by Sāyaṇācārya as *Svapnāvasthā* (i.e. the state of dream). But as per the context it should mean sleep. Here by the word *Svapna* the seer wants to say that during their sleep the sacrificer won't be able to prepare somajuice. This is why the seer is praying to the agent of sleep to keep the sacrificer away from sleep.

The root meaning of the word *Svapna* is 'sleep.' It is derived from the $\sqrt{}$*Svap*.4

The *Amarakoṣa* rightly places sleep *(nidrā)*

at first, in the list of meaning of the word *Svapna*[5].

Hence, the primary meaning of the word *Svapna* (i.e. Sleep) fits to the present context.

In the *Nirukta* of Yāskācārya the word *Svapna* has occurred many times but Niruktakāra has not defined this word etymologically.

The same *mantra (Ṛv. Saṁ. 8.2.18)* also occurs in the *Jaiminiya Saṁhitā (Jai. Saṁ)* 3.7.9., in the *Kauthuma Saṁhitā (Kau. Saṁ.)* 2.31 and in the *Śauṇaka Saṁhitā (Śau. Saṁ)* 20.18.3.

In the *Jaiminiya Brāhmaṇa (Jai. Brā) Brā.* 1.98, 2. 363 and 2.370 the word *Svapna* stands for sleep. In the *Śatapatha Brāhmaṇa (Śat. Brā) Brā* 3.2.2.23, 10.5.2.14, 12.9.2.2; in the *Gopatha Brāhmaṇa (Gopa. Brā.) Brā.* 1.2.2; in the *Upānayana Brāhmaṇa* (Upā. Brā.)* the word *Svapna* also denotes the meaning 'sleep'.

In the *Agnyādheya Brāhmaṇa (Ag. Brā)* 3, the word *Svapna* conveys the meaning of sleep so far the context is concerned. While performing the *Cāturmāsya* sacrifice the sacrificer has to remain awake to establish the sacrificial fire next day. At night sleep may interrupt the continuity of that sacrifice which has been compared with the darkness of night[6].

(ii) Svapna in the sense of Prolonged Or Profound 'Sleep':

By semantic extension, the word *Svapna* also stands for prolonged sleep in some contexts. This can be substantiated by looking into the relevant contexts. For instance, in the *Ṛv. Saṁ.* 2.15.9 we find the seer *Gṛtsamadha* is praising Indra by saying that he killed *Cumuri* and *Dhuni* by casting them into *svapna*. Here the *svapna* is employed as a weapon to kill the demons.7

Sāyanācārya paraphrases *svapna* here as *dīrghanidrā* (i.e. Prolonged sleep). The paraphrase of Sāyana seems to be correct. A question may be raised as to why we don't accept the primary meaning of *svapna* (i.e sleep) here also. The answer will follow from the context. Here, the *Svapna* is employed as a weapon to keep the demons away from the sacrifice, so that they cannot disturb the performance of the sacrifice. Obviously, the performance will take longer time and hence it is necessary that the demons should be kept in a prolonged sleep and not in mere sleep which has shorter duration of time.

Translators like Geldner, Griffith, and Satyaprakash Saraswati have rendered this word into English as 'sleep.' But we think that the English rendering as 'prolonged sleep' will be better.

Veṅkaṭamādhava has commented upon this mantra *'Nidrām nidhāya svapnantam tam dasyun hatavān asi'*. The meaning of this is 'Dasyu was killed by casting him into sleep'. Here also 'prolonged sleep' would be better.

Willson has correctly paraphrased this word as profound sleep (i.e. deep sleep). Because, in deep sleep state mind ceases to function. So the demons won't be able to function as per their desire. In other words, mind is inactive in this state of sleep (i.e. *suṣupti).*

(iii) *Svapna in the sense of 'Dream'*

Ṛsi Rakṣahana approaches Agni for extermination of *svapna* to avert abortion for the sake of off-springs.[8]

As far as the context is concerned here we accept dream, as the meaning of *Svapna*. Because, in dream evil creatures may appear in various forms to beguile women. Dream is the revival of the past images[9]. When one is in deep sleep there is no possibility of dream. Only when deep sleep is yet to come or it is going to disappear generally we dream. To be more exact, apart from the deep sleep state (i.e *Susupti*–state) dream occurs in the mind of a dreamer. Here prayer has been made to avert *svapna*. There is likelihood that during dream women get beguiled and the off-springs in the womb may be hurt or destroyed.

Here *svapna* takes the conventional meaning of dream. In this context also if we accept the earlier two meanings we cannot explain beguiling of the women. Only in dream some frightening scenes can appear by which women may get beguiled and it may cause damage to the womb.

Hence, here *svapna* should mean dream.

We also find an expiation in *Kuṣmāṇḍa Brāhmaṇa (Ku. Brā)* by offering pumpkin as an oblation for the killing of embryo by *svapna*[10].

Here the meaning of *svapna* is dream as the semen may get discharged only during lust-full dream and not during simple sleep or deep sleep. So to check the outflow of semen which may occur in dream but not in sleep or deep sleep this prayer has been made through expiation by the seer.

In the *Śat. Brā., Brā.* 14.7.1.9 denotes the same meaning. It states about the location of the dream-world. It is situated at the junction of the both, the mundane universe and the heaven. Being thereā *tman* can perceive both these world. This idea has been developed further in *Vedānta* Philosophy, where we find the discussion about the dream-world, reality of the entities in that state etc. This state is termed by the word *'Sandhya' (Sandhyastṛtīyam).*

Śat. Brā. 14.7.1.12 states about the soul theory in dream. Here the word *svapna* denotes the meaning of dream. "In dream-state the radiant soul keeps it body aside, remaining awake himself, being possessed of the constant power of vision, watches those who are asleep. Again it comes back to the awaking state."11 *Brā.* 14.7.1.14,17,19, 20 too denote the meaning of the word *svapna* as dream. Before switching over to another semantic change of the word *svapna* I would like to throw some light on how this dream has been elevated to the status of the deity. As it is wellknown, one performs an expiation, in order to satisfy the concerned deity when some shortcomings take place in that performance. Whatever may be the consequence, no one knows that. Still then, after performing the expiation a performer feels satisfaction. Of course, whom we worship he has to be superior one. And having known His functional aspect only we pay our homage to Him. Keeping this view in mind our mentality has developed to treat Him as deity. And hence, in the later *Saṁhitās* dream has got the status of a deity.

Dream has a mythological origin. The references of *Paip. Saṁ* namely, *mantra* No. 3.30.3,4; 17.24.4-11 and *Śau. Saṁ* namely, 6.46. 1.2; 16.5.1, 4-8 clearly corroborate this fact.

Dream has twofold effects-good as well as bad. That is why in the *Śau. Saṁ.* the seer has praised dream by saying that 'Dream is the embryo of the wives of the gods' (i.e. *Devānām patnīnām garbha, Śau. Saṁ* 19.57.3) and further taking dream in a bad sense they have stated that 'Dream is the lair of the Asura' *(Asurasya yonau, Śau. Saṁ* 19.56.1). Again we find the occurence of the word *svapna* (i.e. dream) in many places namely, *Paip. Saṁ* 17.24.1., 3.8.1 etc. in bad sense. Apart from all these there are occurences of the word *svapna* where this word specially conveys the meaning of dream. In these context we have the knowledge of cause-effect relationship between the content of the dream knowledge and the future happenings.[12]

(iv) *Svapna As A Deity:*

In the *kāṭhaka Saṁhitā (kāṭha. Saṁ)* 37.15 We find that in the *Sabā* sacrifice an oblation is being offered to the deity *Svapna* in order to subdue an adversary attack from one who wants to attack the sacrificer while he is asleep.[13]

In the *Mādhyandina Saṁhitā (Mā. Saṁ)* 30.10. We find the seer is praying to the deity *svapna* by offering a blindman as an oblation in the *Puruṣamedha* or human sacrifice.[14] Same *mantra* also occurs in *Taittiriya Brāhmaṇa (Tai. Brā).* 3.4.6. In these *saṁhitās* the word *svapna* stands for deity.

In the *(Śat. Brā.)* we also notice a discussion that being an individual soul *svapna* goes from this world to other world.[15]

Bṛ. Upa. mantra No. 4.3.7 supports this very fact as well.

So from the above discussion it can be summed up that the radical meaning of the word *svapna* was sleep and the meaning got extended in course of time as deep sleep or prolonged sleep, dream and dream as a deity. It is also found that these stages of sleep to dream have developed in the *Ṛv. Saṁ.* gradually and in the later *saṁhitās* it has acquired the meaning of deity also. It may be that after considering the functional aspect of dream it might have been elevated to the status of a deity. The reference of the *Śat. Brā.* 14.7.1.7 attaches Philosophical value to it.

Svapna word occurs only in two *Āraṇyakas* namely, in the *Aitareyāraṇyaka (Ait. Ār)* twice and in the *Śāṅkhyāyana Āraṇyaka (Śāṅ. Ār.)* four times. So in total it occurs six times. Ār. 6.2 in Śāṅ. and the *Ār* 2.4.3 of *Ait* denote 'sleep' and 'deep sleep' respectively as their meaning elsewhere. Apart from these two *Ārs* rest four *svapna* words convey dream as their meaning. The *Ār* 3.2.4 of *Ait.* and the *Ār* 11.4 of *Śāṅ* describe dream as symbol of some future effect. To be more clear, these *Ārs* clearly point out that if a dreamer sees something symbolic in dream, due to that dreamt-event either some auspicious or inauspicious result will come to the dreamer.

NOTES & REFERENCES

* Ghatage, A.M. *An Encyclopedic Dictionary of Sanskrit on*

Historical Principles, p. XXIII.

1. *A Dictionary of Selected synonyms In The Principal Indo-European Languages*, pp. 269
2. Pointed out by Prof. Morgenroth, University of Humboldt., German Democratic Republic (GDR)
3. *Icchanti devāḥ sunvantam na svapnāya spṛhayanti. Yanti pramādam atandrāḥ(Ṛv. Saṁ 8.2.18).*
4. *Svapo nan (Pāṇini* 3.3.91)
5. *Syān nidrā śayanam svapaḥ svapnaḥ saṁveśaḥ iti api (Amarakoṣa 36)*
   * *kāṭhaka-Saṁkalana*, p. 50
6. *Śva ādhāsyamāna rātrim jāgrati tamo vā andham svapnas tamaso eva enam andhaso muñcati* śilpair gāyanti (Ag. Brā. No. 3).
7. Svapnenābhyupyā cumurim Dhunim ca jaghantha dasyum pradabhitibhāvaḥ(Ṛv. Saṁ. 2.15.9).
8. Yastvā svapnena tamasā mohayitvā nipadyate. Prajām yaste jighāṁsati tam ito nāśayāmasi. (Ṛv. Saṁ 10.162. 6)
9. Freud, Sigmund, *The Interpretation of Dreams.*
10. *Om atha kuṣmāṇḍair juhuyād yo' puto iva maṇyet, yad arbā cinam eno bhrūnahatyāyāstasmān mucyeyam iti ayonau vā ryetaḥsiktabān yatra svapnād. Kāṭhaka-saṁkalana*, pp. 87.
11. Translated by Swami Mādhavananda. cf. *Bṛ. Upa* 4.3.11
12. *Svapnam suptvā yadi paśyami pāpam mṛgas srutam yadi dhā vād ajustaṃ. Parikṣavacchakune pāpavādād ayam manir varano vārayātai (Śau. 10.3.6); (paip. 16.63.6)*
13. Prithivyai svāhā antarikṣāya svāhā dive svāhā Kāmāya svāha svapnāya....(Kāṭha. Saṁ. 37.15)
14. *Utsādebhyaḥ kubjam pramuḍe vāmanam dvārbhaḥ srāmam svapnāya andham.... (Mā Saṁ 30.10)*
15. *Katam 'ātmeti, yo 'yam vijñānamayaḥ puruṣaḥ prāṇeṣu*

hṛdyantarjyotiḥsa samānaḥsagnubhau lokau saṁcarati dhyā-yati iva lolāyati iva sadhīḥ svapno bhūtvā imam lokam atikrā mati (*Śat. Brā.* 14.7.1.7).

CHAPTER-III

ANALYSIS OF DREAM IN INDIAN PHILOSOPHICAL LITERATURE

III.0. POSITION IN VEDĀNTA

Analysis of Dream in Advaita School of Philosophy:

The *Bṛhadāraṇyakopaniṣad (Bṛ. Upa.)* says *'Sandhyam tṛtī yam Svapnasthānam iti'* (4.3.9) i.e. 'The dreamstate, which is the third, is at the junction of the two (this and the next world)'. Here doubt arises *'Kim prabodha iva svapne'pi pāramārthikī sṛṣṭir ā hosvid māyāmayīti?'** i.e. 'Whether the creation of the objects in the dream-state is as real as that of the awakened-state or illusory?'

Here the *Pūrvapakṣin* takes a stand and the *Siddhāntin* rejects that after critical examination.

In between this mundane universe and the next world or in other words, at the junction of the awakened-state and the deep sleep-state the dream state is located and this is why it is called *'Sandhyam*[1]. According to the *Pūrvapakṣin* the creation of the objects in this state is real.[2] To support this view he quotes the corroborative evidence from the *Śruti-'Atha rathān rathayogān pathaḥsṛjate iti' (Bṛ. Upa 4.3.10).* The meaning of this sentence is 'He creates the chariot, the animals and the roads'. Here he wants to mean the person himself is the agent of all sorts of creation in the dream-state.[3] This is the stand of the *pūrvapakṣin.* And further, the follower of the ***kaṭha*** recension says that the *jīva* is the creator of the desired objects in **dream**.[4] As a proof for it, they have cited the *Śruti* sentence from **the *kaṭha*** *upaniṣad.* This *Upaniṣad* says- *'Ya eṣa supteṣu jāgarti* ***kāmam*** *kāmam puruṣo nirmimāṇaḥ' (kaṭha. Upa*

5.8). The meaning of this sentence is 'He who remains awake, when these sense organs are asleep, the *puruṣa*, creating the various objects'. Here son etc. are referred by the word *Kāma*. Because they are fit to be desired.[5]

Now some of the follower of this recension raises objection saying that the word *Kāma* should mean special type of desire.[6] But the *Pūrvapakṣin* rules out the objection raised by them by citing the corroborative evidence from *Kaṭhopaniṣad* (verse no. 1.23, 24),[7] where we find the occurrence of the particular word *Kāma* in the sense of 'lovely objects of desire such as sons etc.' and *Prājña* alone can be thought of as the creator of the lovely objects. And hence, the creator is not different from the *Prājña* and it can be verified from both the beginning and the ending portions of the same section of the *Kaṭhopaniṣad*.[8] The description of the *Prājña* begins with the statement 'He whom thou seest as neither this nor that *(kaṭha* 2.14) and ends with the statement 'That indeed is the bright, immortal Brahman, in which all the worlds are contained and beyond which no one goes' *(Kaṭha* 5.8)[9]. So since all these entities in dreamstate are created by *Prājña* all are real like those of the awakened-state.[10]

The *Bṛ. Upa.* goes a step further in identifying both the states when it says 'others, however, say that the dream state of a man is nothing but the waking state, because he sees in dream only those things that he sees in the waking state' *(Bṛ. Upa.* 4.2.14).[11]

Now the *Siddhāntin* refutes the arguments forwarded by the *Pūrvapakṣin* on proper grounds. According to him in the intermediate stage creations of the entities are not real but mere illusion.[12] The dream-entities do not have even slightest reality because of the very fact that the natures of those entities are never fully manifested in the dream.[13]

By the word *'Kārtsnya'* the Bhāṣyakāra clarifies-does not stand for the reality of the entities but it stands for place, time, causation, property and non-contradiction.[14] The nature of the dreamstate does not agree in toto with that of the awakened-state with regard to place, time etc. There can be no appropriate place, time in the dream-state e.g. inside the body there is no enough space for the objects like chariots, horses etc.[15]

The *Pūrvapakṣin* may explain that the soul of the dreamer wanders outside the body in order to adopt things from outside. And in favour of his statement he cites *śruti* sentence which states that 'dream occurs outside the body; away from the nest (body), the immortal moves and goes wherever it likes' *(Bṛ. Upa.* 4.3.12). This is so because without his going out the existence, movement etc. will remain unexplained.[16] The *Siddhāntin* says: It is not possible on the part of a sleeping person who can cover a distance of hundred mile to and fro. Some one may say about his dream that he slept in the land of Kurus and woke up in the land of the *Pañcālas*. But as a matter of fact, the dreamer wakes up in the land of Kurus.[17]

The dreamer may imagin that he is going to a different place, but the persons standing by his side would say that his body is lying in the bed. And dreamer cannot see *svapna* outside his body. At best, the entities which appear real to the dreamer are like real entities. Which he sees in the awakened state, but they themselves are never real entities.[18] *Śruti* also says 'The dreamer moves about, as he likes, within his own body' *(Bṛ. Upa. 2.1.18).* And so, the *śruti* sentence cited by the *Pūrvapakṣin* in order to show that the dreamer moves away from the nest must be interpreted in secondary sense. And taking secondary sense into consideration if we interpret the *śruti* sentence then meaning will be (instead of *'Vahiḥ'* i.e. outside *'Vahiriva'* i.e. like outside) 'He who makes no changes in the body is supposed to make them outside'. The knowledge of the spatial relation which arises in a dream is, therefore, mere illusion.[19]

In dream, the temporal relations with dreamt events do not hold true. As for example, having slept in India at night time a dreamer thinks he is sleeping in daytime outside India. In dream one have the knowledge of a moment as many years.[20]

In dream we also have the perceptual cognition in the absence of casual complexes, namely eyes etc. Since in dream all sense organs cease to function we cannot have the perceptual knowledge of chariot. Because, in dream there cannot be any contact with eyes. Still we have the knowledge of a chariot. Moreover, to prepare a chariot in dream-state we cannot get wood in the twinkling of an eye, which requires more time. And the knowledge of the dream chariot will be contradicted by the knowledge of the chariot in the awakened state. To be more clear, whatever entities the dreamer creates in his dream all will be contradicted after the dreamer gets up. And hence, the contents of dream-knowledge are unreal.[21]

Not only does waking life cancell the dream, but also one event in a dream is cancelled by another. e.g. what appears in dream as chariot turns into a man and man again turns into a tree. The *Siddhāntin* again quotes the *śruti* sentence as a proof where the absence of chariot etc. is obvious in dream *'Na tatra rathā na rathayogā* etc.' *(Bṛ. Upa. 4.3.10)* And hence, what appears in dream is mere illusion.[22] So here the *Siddhāntin* establishes his view by saying that due to the illusory nature of dream it is not true.[23]

But the *Pūrvapakṣin* argues saying that you should not say like this. Because dream is an indicative of future prosperity or future adversity. And to support his view he quotes corrobarative evidence from the *śruti.* As the *Chāndyogyopaniṣad (Chā. Upa.)* says- *'Yadā karmasu kāmyeṣu striyam svapneṣu paśyati samṛddhim tatra jānīyat'* etc. (5.2.9). The meaning of the sentence is 'when a dreamer sees a woman in dream, it is considered as a sign of success in his works desired by him. But the sight of a black man with black teeth indicates earlier death of the dreamer'. And those who are well-versed in chapters dealing with dream say that 'one who sees himself riding on an elephant in dream, is auspicious but to see as riding on a donkey is the symbol of misfortune.'[24]

Some other dreams which are caused by the strength of *mantras,* deties, medicinal herbs etc. are also taken into consideration as real by the *Pūrvapakṣin* so far the indication of future is concerned.[25] But the *Siddhāntin* holds the view that apart from the fact of the indication of some future events, what appears in dream i.e. the content of the dream is false. And the indicator namely, the sight of a woman in dream is unreal. Because it is contradicted by our experience when the dreamer gets up. And hence, dreams are nothing but mere illusion.[26] Therefore, the *Upaniṣadic* passage cited under sutra No. 1 of this *adhyāya* (3.2.1) must be interpreted in secondary sense.

As for example, we say generally that plough carries cows but the moment we glance at the contrary knowledge arises. Likewise, having slept he himself creates chariot etc. but in the true sense in sleep we cannot create anything.

Here *Bhāṣyakāra's* intension is that, though sometimes the dream produces joy, fear etc. in the mind of the dreamer, but it is caused by the merits and demerits and not by those entities since they are unreal.[27]

Moreover, the knowledge acquired in the awakened state depends upon the contact of the objects with the sense organs and upon the auxiliary causes like the light of the sun etc. But the dream world is totally different from the waking world. Dream world is beyond the range of the sun rays or moonlight. In dream we cognise the entities because of the self-luminious nature of the *'Ātman'*. This fact is indicated by the *śrutis* pertaining to dream and dream knowledge.[28]

If we hold that the creations of the chariots etc. in the dreamstate are true on the ground of *śruti* then it would become difficult to justify the self-illumining character of the *Ātman*. Thus, the absence of the chariots etc. in the statement 'There are no chariots' etc. (*Bṛ Upa.* 4.3.10) is real description of the dream state and 'He creates the chariot etc.' (*Bṛ Upa.* 4.3.10). 'He creates all the objects of desire' (*Kaṭha* 5.8) should be taken in the primary sense and the creation or presence of those entities in the dream should be taken in the secondary sense. This is how the vedic statements of the creation of entities in dream is explained.[29]

If we postulate that *Prājña* is the creator of all these entities namely, dream chariot etc,[30] it is not true because, *śruti* says *'svayam vihatyā svayam ninirmāya svena bhāsā svena jyotiṣā prasvapiti'* (*Bṛ. Upa.* 4.3.9). This *śruti* means 'He (*Jīva*) himself puts the body aside and himself creates (a dream body in its place), revealing his own lustre by his own light and dreams'. There is another *śruti* from the *Kaṭhopanisad 'Ya eṣa supteṣu jāgrati'* (*Kaṭha.* 5.8). All these go to prove that *Jīva* is the creator of all dream entities.[31]

It comes immediately after as a continuation of the verse just quoted, the same being is described as the 'bright, immortal Brahman'. Since *Jīva* has not been conceived separately from the *Brahman* and that too also supported by the *Chāndyogyopaniṣad 'Tat tvamasi'*, means 'you are that' (*Chā. Upa* 6.9.4). We may also say *Prā jña*, the lord of all, because of its omnipresence.[32] By this we maintain that the creation in dream is not as real as sky etc. The later also is not real says the *Brahmah sūtra (B.S.)* 2.1.14.

The duration of both the states namely, the awakened state and the dreamstate are relative one. The former one lasts till the knowledge of Brahman and later is sublated daily by the waking life. And hence, the special characteristics of dream is mere illusion.[33]

Now the *Pūrvapakṣin* brings forth the argument in a modified form by saying that as both the spark and the fire possess, in common, the power to burn and to give light, likewise *Jīva* and the *Īśvara* possess in common the knowledge and all sorts of properties. So it is likely that the individual soul may create from his mere desire real things like chariot due to his *Jñanaiśvarya.* [34]

In reply to this someone says it is true that as part is related to whole likewise, *jīva* is related to *Īśvara* but their properties are altogether different. [35] Again the *Pūrvapakṣin* raises question that you do not like to accept equal properties of both the *jīva* as well as the *Īśvara.*[36]

Now the *Pūrvapakṣin's* statement is being refuted by the *Siddhāntin* on this ground. Divine attributes, although exist potentially, are hidden in the individual soul on account of *avidyā.* And just as the sight of a blindman may be restored by means of medicine, likewise if a man wins the grace of god by constant meditation on Him, the divine qualities in him may become manifest and enable him to dispel his ignorance. In the absence of devotion and grace on the otherhand, the qualities don't manifest themselves.[37] And hence, the bondage and liberation of a man are said to be dependent on god.[38] So in other words, bondage means the ignorance of the real nature of god and after realisation (of the real nature of god) the salvation will follow.[39] To corroborate this fact the *Siddhāntin* quotes *śruti* sentence from *Śvetāśvataropaniṣad (Śvetā.Upa.)* '*Jñatva* devam sarvapāśāpahāniḥ-kṣīṇaiḥ kleśair janma mṛtyu prahāṇiḥ'. The meaning of this sentence is 'After the real knowledge of god, all fetters fall off, sufferings and the cycle of births and deaths come to an end', and by meditation on god the devotee acquires a unique glory which makes him completely satisfied.[40] The *Siddhāntin* again wants to know how the *Jīva* is the part of the highest *Ātman.* If we conceive *Jīva* and the highest reality as one and the same then as spark of fire manifests its power of burning and light similarly the *Jīva* may manifest its hidden qualities.[41]

What you say is true. But that fading away of *Jñāna* is possible only when the soul of a person comes in contact with the *Upādhis* of the body and through that with organs, mind, intellect, object, pain etc.[42] These are the names and forms arising out of *avidyā* and through all these we get erroneous notion in the soul that these are not distinct from soul. Naturally the divine qualities of the soul are hidden by these in the same manner as the power of the fire is hidden namely to light and to burn in the churning wood or as it is covered by ashes.[43]

And because of the association with factor like body which has name and form, *Jīva* is devoid of knowledge and all sorts of properties which *Paramātman* has. To be more exact, *avidyā* causes *nāma* and *rūpa*. When the *Jīva* gets associated with body, his association with the body causes illusion and because of this mental creation occurs.[44] But it is impossible to hold that soul and god are separate. The use of *'Vā'* in the *sūtra 'dehayogādvā'* is to remove the doubt that Jīva is not different from *Īśvara*. Actually speaking here he wants to mean *'Jīvabrahmaivanāparaḥ'* i.e. *Jīva* and *Īśvara* are one and the same and this is the force of *'Vā'*[45].

Now, the *Siddhāntin* says: why unnecessarily are you trying to identify *Jīva* and *Īśvara?* Let ther be difference between the two, since *Jiva* doesn't possess *Jñānaiśvarya*. What is the need of postulating the association of body etc.? [46]

The *Pūrvapakṣin* says: your suggestion cannot be accepted because, it is difficult to establish that *Jīva* is different from *Īśvara*. He quotes the corroborative evidence from the *Śruti* where *Jīva* and *Īśvara* both are identified. *'Seyam devataikṣata' (Chā. Upa.* 6.3.2) begins with this sentence and ends with *'Anena Jīvenātmanā' 'nupraviśya' (Chā. Upa.* 6.9.4). Here, *Ātman* and *Jīva* are identical. Again *'Tat satyam sa ātmā tattvamasi śvetketo' (Chā. Upa. 6.9.4)* refers to *Jīva* as identical with *Īśvara*.[47]

As a matter of fact, *Jīva* and *Īśvara* are one and the same. The minute difference is this that one has body and other doesn't. And due to the association with the body *Jīva* is devoid of *Jñanaiśvarya*. Therefore, *sāṅkalpikīsṛṣṭi* doesn't fit into the Jīva.[48] If at all it is accepted that *Jīva* were to create entities like chariot etc. in dream he would have never produced unpleasant and inauspicious events in his dream, because it is our common experience that no one desires anything harmful for his own sake.[49]

As for the *Śruti* passage *(Bṛ. Upa.* 4.3.14) which, according to the *Pūrvapakṣin*, teaches us that the dreaming state is as real as the waking state since the dreamer sees in a dream exactly the same thing as he sees in the awakened-state. The *Siddhāntin* says that the statement of the *Śruti* is not to certify that the dream-entities are real. If dreams were as real as the waking state then we cannot establish the self-luminating nature of the *Ātman*. Moreover, *śruti* also points out the absence of the entities like chariot etc. in dream (*Bṛ. Upa.* 4.3.10).[50] And hence, dream entities are unreal because these are caused by the *Vāsanās* of the awakened-state and appear in our dream in that form. Actually speaking, these are illusory and not real.[51]

NOTES & REFERENCES

* Vide the commentary of Śaṅkara on *Brahmasūtras (B.S.)* 3.2. 1-6 as follows:

1. Dvayorlokasthānayoḥ prabodha saṁprasādasthānayor vā saṁdhau bhavatīti saṁdhyam.
2. *Tasmin saṁdhye sthāne tathyarūpaiva sṛṣṭirbhavitum arhati.*
3. Sa hi kartā iti ca upasaṁhārād evam evāvagamyate.
4. Api ca eke śākhino'smin eva saṁdhye sthāne kāmānām nirmā tāram ātmānam āmananti.
5. Putrādayaśca tatra kāmā abhipreyante-kāmyanta iti
6. *Nanu kāmaśabdena icchāviśeṣā eva ucyeran.*
7. 'Śatāyuṣaḥ putrapautrān vṛṇīṣva' (Kaṭha. Upa) iti prakṛtyānte 'kāmānām tvā kāmabhājam karomi' (Kaṭha. Upa. 1.24) iti prakṛteṣu tatra tatra putrādisu kāmaśabdasya prakṛtvāt.
8. Prājñam ca enam nirmātāram prakaraṇa vākyaśeṣābhyām pratīmaḥ.
9. Prājñasya hi idam prakaraṇam- 'Anyatra dharmād anyatra adharmād.... yat tat paśyasi tadvada' (Kaṭha. 2.14) ityādi. Tadviṣaya eva ca vākyaśeṣo'pi- 'Tad eva śukram tadbrahma tadeva amṛtam ucyate. Tasmin lokāḥ śritāḥ sarve tad unātya iti kaścana' (Kaṭha. 5.8) iti.
10. Prājñakartṛkā ca sṛṣṭiḥ tathyarūpa samadhigatā jāgaritāśrayā,

tathā svapnāśrayā' pi sṛṣṭir bhavitum arhati.

11. 'Atha khalu āhur jāgaritadeśa evāsyaiṣa iti yāni hi eva jāgrat paśyati tāni suptaḥ' (Bṛ. Upa. 4.3.14) iti svapna jāgaritayoḥ samānanyāyatām śrāvayati.

12. Tu śabdaḥ pakṣam vyāvartayati. Na etad asti yaduktam saṁdhye sṛṣṭiḥ pāramārthikiti, māyā iva saṁdhye sṛṣṭiḥ.

13. Na paramārtha gandhyo'pi asti, kārtsnena na abhivyakta svarupatvāt.

14. Na hi kārtsnyena paramārtha vastudharmeṇa abhivyakta-svarūpaḥ svapnaḥ. Deśakāla nimitta saṁpattir abādhaśca.

15. Na hi paramārtha vastuviṣayāṇi deśakālanimittāni abādhaśca svapne saṁbhāvyante, na tāvat svapne rathādīnām ucito deśaḥ saṁbhavati.

16. Darśayati ca śrutir bahir dehāt svapnam-'bahiṣkulāyādamṛta ścaritvā sa iyate' mṛto yatra kāmam' (Bṛ Upa. 4.3.12) iti sthiti gati pratyaya bhedaśca na aniṣkrānte jantau sāmañ jasyam aśnuvīteti.

17. Na iti ucyate. Na hi suptasya jantoḥ kṣaṇamātreṇa yojanaśatā ntaritam deśaparjetum viparjetum ca tataḥ sāmarthyam sambhāvyate. Kvacicca pratyāgamana varjitam svapnam śrā vayati-kuruṣu aham adya śāyano nidrayā' bhiplutaḥ svapne pañcālān abhigataśca eṣu pratibudhaśceti. Dehācced apeyāt pañcāleṣu prativudhyet na tānasāvabhigata iti kuruṣu eva tu pratibhudhyate.

18. Yena ca ayam dehena deśāntaram aśnuvāno manyate tamanye parśvasthāḥ śayanadeśa eva paśyanti. Yathābhūtāni ca svam deśāntarāni svapne paśyati na tāni tathābhūtāni eva bhavanti. Paridhāvaṁścet paśyet jāgradvad vastubhūtam artham ākalayet.

19. Darśayati ca śrutir antareva dehe svapnam-'sa yatra etat svapnayācarati' iti upakramya 'sva śarīre yathākāmam parivartate' (Bṛ. Upa. 2.1.18) iti. Ataśca, śruti upapatti virodhād bahiṣkulāya srutir gauṇī vyākhyātavyā-vahiriva kulāyād

amṛtascaritveti. Yo hi vasannapi śrīre na tena prayojanam karoti sa vahiriva śrīrād bhavatīti; sthitigati pratyaya bhedo'pi evam sati vipralambha eva abhi upagantavyaḥ.

20. Kālavisaṁvādo'pi ca svapne bhavati-rajanyām supto vāsaram bhārate varse manyate. Tathā muhūrta mātravartini svapne kadācid vahuvarṣa pūgān ativāhayati.

21. Nimittāni api ca svapne na vuddhaye karmaṇe va ucitāni vidyante. karaṇopasaṁhāraddhi na asya rathādi grahanāya cakṣuradīni santi. Rathādi nirvartane'pi kuto' sya nimeṣa mā trena sāmarthyam dārūṇi vā. Bādhyante ca ete rathādayaḥ svapnadṛṣṭāḥ∫ prabodhe, svapna eva ca ete sulabhavādhā bhavanti, ādyantayor vyabhicāra darśanāt.

22. Ratho' yam iti hi kadācit svapne nirdhāritaḥ

kṣaṇena manuṣya saṁpadyate, manusyo' yam iti

nirdhāritaḥkṣaṇena vṛkṣa. Spaṣṭam ca abhāvam rathādīnā m svapne śrāvayati śāstram- 'Na tatra rathā na rathayogā ṇa Panthāno bhavanti' (Bṛ 4.3.10) ityādi. Tasmād māyāmatram svapna darśanam.

23. Māyāmatratvat tarhi na kaścit svapne paramārtha gandho' stī ti.

24. Na iti ucyate sucakaśca hi svapno bhavati bhaviṣyatoḥsādhu asādhunoḥ∫ tathā hi śruyate-'Yadā karmasu kāmyeṣu striyam svapneṣu paśyati samṛdhim tatra jānīyat tasmin svapna nidarśane' (Chā. Upa. 5.2.9). 'Tathā puruṣam kṛsṇam kṛsṇadantam paśyati sa enam hanti'. Ityevamādibhiḥsvapnair cirajī vitvam ā vedyata iti śrāvayati, ācakṣate ca svapnādhyāyavidaḥ- 'kuñjar ārohaṇa ādīnī svapne dhanyāni kharayānādīnya dhanyāni' iti.

25. Mantra devatā dravya viśeṣa nimittāśca kecit svapnāḥ satyā rtha gandhino bhavantīti manyante.

26. Tatrāpi bhavatu nāma sūcyamānasya vastunaḥ satyatvam, sucakasya tu strī darśnāder bhavati eva vaitathyam, bādhya mānatvāt iti abhiprāyaḥ. Tasmādupapannam svapnasya māyā

mātratvam.

27. Yad uktam 'āha hi' iti tadevam sati bhāktam vyākhyātavyam. Yathā lāṅgalam gavādīn udvahatīti nimittamātratvād evam ucyate, nanu pratyakṣam eva lāṅgalam gavādīnudvahati. Evam nimittamātratvāt supto rathādīn sṛjate sa ḥi kartā iti ca ucyate, na tu pratyakṣameva supto rathādīn sṛjati. Nimittatvam tu asya rathādi pratibhāna nimitta moda trāsādi darśanāt tannimittabhūtayoḥ sukṛta duṣkṛtayoḥ kartṛtveneti vaktavyam.

28. Api ca jagarite viṣayendriya saṁyogād ādityādi jyotir vyatikarā cca ātmanaḥsvayamjyotiṣtvam durvivecanam iti tad vivecanā ya svapna upanyastaḥ

29. Tatra yadi rathādisṛṣṭivacanam śrutyā nīyate, tadāsvayam jyotiṣṭvam na nirṇītam syāt. Tasmād rathādi abhāvavacanam śrutya, rathādi sṛṣṭivacanam tu bhāktyeti vyākhyeyam.

30. Yad api uktam-'Prājñamenam nirmātāram āmananti' iti

31. Tad api asat, śrutyāntare 'svayam vihatya svayam ninirmāya svena bhāsā svena jyotiṣā prasvapiti' (Bṛ. Upa. 4.3.9) iti jīvavyā pāra śravaṇāt. Iha api 'ya eṣa suptesu jāgarti' (Kaṭha. 5.8) iti prasiddha anuvādāt jīva eva ayam kāmānām nirmātā saṁkī rtyate.

32. Tasya tu vākyaśeṣena tad eva śukram tadbrahma iti. jīvabhāve vyavartya Brahmabhāva upadiśyate- 'Tat tvam asi' (Chā. Upa 6.9.4) ityadivad iti na Brahmaprakaraṇam virudhyate. Na ca asmābhiḥ svapnepi prājña vyavahāraḥ pratiṣidhyate; tasya sarveśvaratvāt sarvāsu avasthāsu adhiṣṭhatṛtva upapatteḥ.

33. Pāramārthikastu na ayam saṁdhyāśrayaḥ svargo vidyadādi sargavad iti etāvad pratipādyate. Na ca viyadādisargasya api ātyantikam satyatvam asti.

Pratipāditam hi 'Tadananyatvam ārambhaṇaśabdādibhyaḥ '(B. S 2.1.14) iti atra samastasya prapañcasya māyāmā tratvam. Prāk tu Brahma ātmatva darśanād viyadādi prapañco vyavasthitarūpo bhavati. Saṁdhyāśrayastu prapañca pratidinam bādhyata iti. Ato vaiśeṣikam idam saṁdhasya māyāmātratvam uditam.

34. Tatra evam sati yathā'gni visphuliṅgayoh samāne dahanaprakāśanaśaktī bhavata evam jīva Īśvarayor api jñānaiśvarya śaktī, tataśca jīvasya jñanaiśvaryavaśāt saṁkalpikī svapne rathādi sṛṣṭir bhaviṣyatīti.

35. Atra ucyate-satyapi jīva īśvarayoh aṁśā-aṁśibhāve pratyakṣam eva jīvasya īśvara viparita dharmatvam.

36. Kim punar jīvasya īśvara samāna dharmatvam nāsti eva?

37. Na nāsti eva. vidyamānamapi tat tirohitam avidyādi vyavadhā nāt. Tat punaḥ tirohitam sat parameśvaram abhidhyāyato yatamānasya jantor vidhūta dhvāntasya timir atiraskṛta eva dṛkśaktir auṣadha vīryādi īśvara prasādāt saṁsiddhasya kasyacid eva āvirbhavati na svabhāvata eva sarveṣām jantūnā m.

38. Tatoḥ hī īśvarāddhetorasya jīvasya bandha mokṣau bhavataḥ

39. Īśvara svarūpa aparijñānād bandhastatsvarūpa parijñānāt tu moksa.

40. Tathā ca śrutiḥ'jñātvā devam sarvapāśā pahāniḥ kṣīṇaiḥ kleśairjanmamṛtyu prahāṇiḥ tasyābhidhyānāt tṛtīyam dehabhede viśvaiśvaryam kevala āptakāmaḥ' (Śvetā. Upa. 1.11) iti evam ādyā.

41. Kasmāt punar jīvaḥ paramātmāṁśa eva saṁstiraskṛtajñān-aiśvaryo bhavati? Yuktam tu jñānaiśvaryayor atiraskṛtatvam visphuliṅgasya eva dahana prakāśanayor iti.

42. Satyam eva etat; so' pi tu jīvasya jñānaiśvarya tirobhāvo dehayogād deha indriya manaḥ buddhi viṣayavedanādi yogād bhavati.

43. Asti ca atra upamā yathā agner dahana prakāśana saṁpannasyāpi araṇigatasya dahana prakāśane tirohite bhavato yathā vā bhasmācchannasya.

44. Evam abidyā prati upasthāpita nāma-rūpakṛta-dehād upādhi-yogād tad viveka bhramakṛto jīvasya jñāna-aiśvarya tirobhāvaḥ

45. Vā śabdo jīva Īśvarayor anyatva āśaṅkā vyavṛttarthaḥ

46. Nanu anya eva jīva īśvarādstu, tirskṛta jñānaiśvaryatvāt; kim dehayoga kalpanayā?

47. Na iti ucyate. Na hi anyatvam jīvasya īśvarād-upapadyate 'seyam devataikṣata' (Chā. Upa 6.3.2) iti upakramya 'Anena jī vena ātmanā 'nupraviśya' (Chā Upa. 6.3.2) iti ātmā śabdena jī vasya parāmarśat. 'Tat satyam sa ātmā tattvam asi svetketo' (Chā. Upa 6.9.4) iti ca jīvāyopadiśati īśvarātmatvam.

48. Ataḥ 'nanya eva īśvarād jīvaḥ san dehayogād tirohita jñā naiśvaryo bhavati. Ataśca na sāṁkalpikī jīvasya svapne rathā di sṛṣṭir ghatate.

49. Yadi ca sāṁkalpiki svapne rathādi sṛṣṭiḥsyād eva aniṣṭam kaś-cit svapnam paśyet. Na hi kaścid aniṣṭam saṁkalpayate.

50. Yat punaruktam-Jāgaritadeśa śrutiḥsvapnasya satyatvam sthā payatīti, na tat sāmyavacanam satyatvabhiprāyam; svayam jyotiṣṭva virodhāt, śrutaiva ca svapne rathādi abhāvasya darśitatvāt.

51. Jāgarita prabhava-vāsanā nimittatvāttu svapnasya tattulya nirbhāsatvābhiprāyam tat. Tasmād upapannam svapnasya māyāmātratvam.

Vācaspati on Dream-knowledge:

Vācaspati commented upon the *Śaṅkarabhāṣya (śan.bhā).*On the Brahmasūtras (B.Ss.). His commentary is known by the name of *'Bhāmati'(Bhām.)*While commenting on the 'Kiṁprabodha iva svapne'pi pāramārthiki sṛṣṭiḥ āhosvid māyāmayiti?' under B.S. 3. 2.1. he initiates the dicussion whether the creation of the objects in dream can be considered to be real like the awakened-state or illusory?

The established view is that in both the states namely, the waking state as well as in dream state, whatever entity other than the absolute reality is found to exist is not real but illusory.[1]. There is only the difference in degree of the duration of existence between waking state and that of the dream state and that difference is simply this that even the entities of the waking state lose their reality after the person identifies himself with his 'Self' (i.e. the Brahman).[2]

In other words, it is a matter of duration of time that alone varies. At this stage *Pūrvapakṣin* argues that no knowledge, be it the knowledge in the dream state, or in the waking state, is false and hence, the objects of such true knowledges have to be real. Therefore, the objects of a dream-knowledge have to be real.[3] To establish this the pūrvapakṣin employ's the following inference:

(i) The object of any knowledge is real.

(ii) Because, it appears in its knowledge in its own form.

(iii) It has not been observed so far that the object of knowledge does not appear in its own form in its cognition.

(iv) The present knowledge is also of the same class of knowledge.

(v) Therefore, its object is real.[4]

The *Siddhāntin* points to a contrary case, in which the object appears in a different form. For instance, the rope appears as a snake. In other words according to the *Siddhāntin* there can be contradiction between two cognitions.[5] To this, the *Purvapakṣin* reacts by saying that it is not true to say that under any conditions two cognitions will contradict.[6] But it is only proper to say that the two cognitions contradict only if a cognition having one and the same object terminates in revealing two different objects.[7] After one decides that one out of the two cognitions is stronger and the other one is weaker, the two cognitions are said to be related through the contradictor-contradicted relationship.[8]

Under this criterion, what you consider to be the contradictory cognition is not a contradictory cognition-tells the *Pūrvapakṣin*. Because, in the case under review, the object is not one and the same. Since we can distinguish the objects of the cognition of awakened state and those of the dream state on the basis of the difference of time,[9] namely, the awakened state time and dream state time, dream knowledge and the knowledge of the awakened state are not contradictory. No one will say that the knowledge of milk contradicts the knowledge of curd prepared out of the same milk. Since, though it was milk when it was known as milk, in course of time it has become curd.[10] And so, since the objects of the two cognitions are not the same they are not contradictory.

Similarly, when one sees silver and later on sees the Conch-shell, the two cognitions cannot be said to be contradictory simply because the seen silver becomes conch-shell in course of time.[11]

Or, we can also argue that one object can appear in various forms.[12] One particular causal complex will reveal one particular form of the same object and the other complex, the other.[13]

For instance, when a person moves under the sun and gets tired his eyes being associated with the rays of the sun reveal the object as silver. But a person who is not under that situation sees the object as Conch-shell only, under normal light required to see an object.[14]

Likewise, in day light a blue-reddish lotus is perceived as blue one, but the same lotus is perceived as red under the light of lamp.[15]

In the same manner, a chariot seen in the dream is not seen in the awakened state because the dream-chariot is visible only when there is sleep and not otherwise. Similarly, the chariot seen in the awakened state is not seen in the dream simply because, there is no awakened state, when one is asleep.[16] Thus, a particular perception can take place in the presence of a particular causal complex only. The sleep, awakened state, light, rays of the sun etc, are considered to be various causal complexes. One causal complex may be operative in the dream state and the other in the awakened state.

Therefore, there is no contradiction between two cognitions ofthe awakened state and the dream state. And if this is true, the objects of both the cognitions have to be real.

Since the objects of the cognition of both the states are found to appear in their own form there is no criterion to decide why the objects of the awakened state should be real and those of the dream state unreal.[17]

Thus the conclusive inference will be as follows:

(i) The dream-cognition about which controversies have arisen are real.

(ii) Because they are cognitions.

(iii) Like the cognitions of pillar etc. at the awakened state.[18]

To support this inference the *Pūrvapakṣin* quotes dream corroborative evidence from the *Śruti.* The *Śruti* says *'Atha rathān raṭhayogān pathaḥsṛjate iti'.* The meaning of this sentence is 'He creates the chariots, the animals and the roads'. The *Pūrvapakṣin* anticipates that the Siddhāntin may interpret this *śruti* in a different way by taking *sṛjate* in the secondary sense and in that case the entities seen in the dream may not be real.[19]

Anticipating this the *Pūrvapakṣin* rules out this interpretation by saying that one cannot take the meaning of *sṛjate* as secondary or imposed one, since the same form is found to occur in many places in the primary sense and since there are other proofs to corroborate this primary sense. Hence, the suprimacy of the *Śruti* remains intact. And inorder to maintain this suprimacy of the *Śruti* one is required to interpret the sentence *'Na tatra ratha'* etc. in the secondary sense.[20]

Thus the meaning of that *śruti* will be the entities seen in the dream state are not fit to be seen in the awakened state. And it does not mean that those entities like the Chariots etc. of the dream state are not real.[21] And this is the reason why two sentences describing the *Prājña* as the creator have been quoted from two different *Upaniṣads* demonstrating the identical meaning. On this very ground the entities are created by the *Prājña* himself one should treat those entities as real like sky etc.[22]

One need not doubt that since these entities are created by *jīva* actually speaking they should not be treated as being created by *prā jña*. Because this description occurs in the context of *prājña* only. [23]

Even if it is stated that the entities are created by *jiva, still, since jī va* is not conceived as different from the *Prājña*. [24]

Hence, the entities of the dream state have to be real.

Moreover, it is our experience that sometimes we get the knowledge of entities in dream which correspond to the entities of the awakened state.[25]

For example, one Priyavrata dreams that a Brahmin wearing white garment and bearing white garland and mark of the paste of sandal-wood tells him oh Priyabrata, the king will honour you on the fifth day of your dream, early morning. After coming back to the awakened state and having observed that he is being honoured by the king on the fifth-day, he believes the dream-knowledge to be real.[26]

All these go to prove that the entities revealed in the dream are real one. Therefore, the creations in intermediate stage are true.[27]

To this the *siddhāntin* has the following reply. The dream-entities are mere illusions since dream does not manifest any entity in its true or actual form.[28]

To be more exact, it is not true that a piece of silver gets transformed into a conch-shell in the same sense as milk gets transformed into curd.[29]

Even if one keeps silver-pots in the house of god, forever, they will never be transformed into conch-shell.[30]

It is also not true that while a person sees silver in a conch-shell another person will not perceive silver there unless his sense-organs are disturbed.[31]

It is also not proper to say that one single entity can have double form and they will be realised differently in different situations. Due to the causal complexes, sometimes a single substance appears in dual form. e.g. the mirage may appear before us like water under one causal complex and as rays of the sun under another causal complex.[32]

Because, had the mirage been actual water, then it must perform the function of water namely, the quenching of thirst. Similarly it should have performed the function of illuminating the objects.[33]

But it is not a fact that someone's thirst is quenched by mirage. Water cannot have both the properties namely, quenching the thirst and not quenching thirst. Because, if being water does not perform the function of quenching the thirst it can no longer be designated as water.[34]

Morever, in order to justify the knowledge of water after seeing the mirage, you are accepting double form of the mirage, but even if that is accepted, it cannot establish that. It can be explained as follows:

If one knows that 'that water is incapable of quenching thirst, he will not go to fetch that even if he is very thirsty'. But as a matter of fact, he does run after the mirage for getting water. If you say that he runs after the mirage considering it capable of quenching the thirst although it is not so, then what is the harm in treating the knowledge of water after seeing the mirage as erroneous one?[35]

Why unnecessarily are you trying to postulate another type of erroneous cognition.[36]

The knowledge of water after seeing the mirage is not like the knowledge of curd when one also knows that the curd is prepared out of milk. It is also not like the knowledge of a teacher who also happens to be maternal uncle of the knower and also a brahmin. Where all the entities are cognised separately. In short, it is not a *samūhālambana* (multi-qualificand) cognition but in reality the knowledge of mirage and that of water are mutually contradictory.[37]

There too, the knowledge of silver is a knowledge 'to be contradicted' and it arose first and the knowledge of conch-shell is a knowledge which contradicts the earlier knowledge of silver. This is true because the knowledge which contradicts requires its objects namely, the knowledge which is to be contradicted.[38]

Prior to the knowledge of silver since there is no knowledge which can reveal conch-shell, the conch-shell is not known at all and what is not known cannot be negated and therefore the fact remains that the knowledge of conch-shell negates the silver, known by the earlier knowledge. This fact can be corroborated by one's own experience.[39]

The same is supported by the following statement: The earlier knowledge arises without concelling the latter knowledge since the later knowledge has not arisen yet and without cancelling the earlier knowledge the latter never arises.[40]

It is also not proper to argue as follows:

The knowledge which reveals silver at present time cannot be contradicted by a knowledge of conch-shell of that time without making the future time as its object, because no contradiction takes place between two cognitions at two different times.[41]

Accepting that the perception of silver does not reveal the future time of the silver, but as the ground for its utility causes the knowledge of its being useful by inference. Similarly, the inference will cause the knowledge of the continuous existence of silver till the knowledge of conch-shell, which is the obstructing knowledge, does not arise.[42] The following will be the form of such inference:

A silver, in the absence of the knowledge of conch-shell, continues, to exist, since it is a silver, like a silver which was known as silver and recognised as silver.[43]

Thus, a perception of silver will reveal a durable silver only. And as a result of it, the existence of silver will pervade the time of the future knowledge of conch-shell. And thus there is contradiction and hence the knowledge of conch-shell will cancell the knowledge of silver.[44] The same analysis is presented in the following verse:

When silver is known it is known as durable one and hence it continues to exist till the knowledge of the conch-shell.[45] Someone interprets as follows:

'(When silver is known) it is known as durable by perception'. But this interpretation is not proper. Because, if being 'durable' (*cirasthāyitva*), is taken to stand for 'capability' it is not true because 'capability' is a *'sakti* which is beyond of the range of our senseorgans.[46]

Well, if you take that *cirasthāyitva* to mean 'being pervader of future time', i.e., being present in future time also. That is also not proper. Because, there cannot be present contact with future object and since pervaderness is qualified by this fact, this too goes beyond the range of perception.[47]

It is also not like the knowledge of recognition or recollection where even a past entity becomes the object of perception. Because in the case of recollection, the impression left behind by the past experience continues to exist in the soul, but no such impression is available here which can generate the perception of future silver in this case. And therefore, by saying *'cirasthāyīti gṛhyate'* What he means is 'because of repeated experience, after the perception of silver, there arises a quicker perception which is helped by an inference:'[48]

This is why, without considering the minute difference in the intermediate duration of time, the Buddhists say--The content of a perceptual cognition is of two types namely, that which is cognised and that which is determinately revealed. The first one is known as *svalakṣana* and the second one the *santāna or a chain of svalakṣanas.*[49]

By all this, that a dream knowledge is false is explained.[50] As regards the *pūrvapakṣin's* reference to some cases of corroboration between the objects of dream cognition and those of the normal cognition, the *siddhāntin* points out that those cases can be treated as cases of mere chance. And hence, the example of Priyavrata etc., given by *pūrvapakṣin* is not dependable. Because many a time dream objects are not corroborated.[51]

Such contradictions between the object of dream and those of awakened state have been made quite explicit by Śaṅkarācārya himself by saying that the objects of dream do not appear in their whole form. An example of contradiction given the *Bhāsya* is having slept at night in India, a dreamer dreams that he is sleeping outside India (i.e. Western Country) in day time.[52]

So, this is no one to one correspondence between the content of dream-knowledge and that of the awakened state.

Therefore, dream cognitions are false.

Someone suggests that dream-knowledge is an indicative of future events. It is true in form but what is shown these are not true. Since the objects of our dream-behaviour disappear after we get up.[53] If someone postulates that the *Īśvara (Prājña)* is the creator of all those dream entities namely, the Chariot etc. then it will not be proper. Because in that case those entities should be as real as the sky etc. which are created by *Īśvara.* But this is not corroborated by our direct experience. Therefore, the dream-entities are not real. In other words, if someone claims that the dream-entities are real because they are created by *Prājña,* it is not true, because the *Prājña* cannot be the creator of those entities. Had he been the creator of those entities they would have been experienced directly as the sky etc. But since it is not the case and since the dream-entities do not continue to exist after one gets up from the dream, it cannot be held that those dream-entities are created by *Prājña* and since these are not created by *Prājña*, they have to be accepted as being created by *Jīva* and as such those dream-entities have to be unreal.[54]

NOTES AND REFERENCES

* Vide *Bhā* on B.S.Ś. No, 3.2.1-6 as follows:

1. *Jāgrat svapnāvasthāgatayor ubhayor api sargayor māyā mayatvam.*
2. *Jāgrat sṛṣṭi Brahma ātmabhāvasākṣātkārāt prāganuvartate.*
3. *Iha hi sarvāṇi eva mithyā jñānāni udāharanam, teṣām satyatvam pratijñāyate, prakṛta upayogitayā tu svapnajñānam udā hṛtaṁ.*
4. *Jñānam yam artham avabodhayati sa tathaiveti yuktam; tathā bhāvasya jñānārohāt, atathātvasya tu apartiyamānsya tathā bhāva-prameya-virodhena kalpana anāspadatvāt.*
5. *Bādhakapratyayād atathātvamiti cet.*
6. *Na, tasya bādhakatvāt asiddheḥ*
7. *Samānagocare hi viruddhārtha upasaṁhāriṇi jñāne virudhyate.*
8. *Balavad abalavatvaniścayācca bādhyabādhakabhāvam pratipadyete.*
9. *Na ca iha samānaviṣayatvam: Kālabhedena vyavasthā upā patteḥ*
10. *Yathā hi kṣīram dṛstam kālāntare dadhi bhavet.*
11. *Evam rajatam dṛtam kalāntare suktiḥ bhavet.*
12. *Nānārūpam Vā tadvastu.*
13. *Sāmagrībhedādvā kālabhedādvā virodhābhāvaḥ*
14. *Tad yasya tīvra ātapaklānti sahitam cakṣu sa tasya rajatarū patām gṛṇhāti. Yasya tu kevalam ālokamātra upakṛta, sa tasya*

eva śuktirūpatām gṛṇhāti.

15. *Evam utpalamapi nilalohitam divā saurībhirbhābhir abhivyaktam nīlatayā gṛhyate, pradipābhivyaktam tu naktam lohitatayā.*

16. *Evam asatyām nidrāyām sato'pi rathādīn na gṛṇhāti, nidrāṇastu gṛṇhāti iti.*

17. *Dvayorapi svagocaracāritaya samānatvena vinigamanā hetorabhāvāt.*

18. *Tat siddhametat. Vivādāspadam pratyayāh. samyañca, pratyayatvat, jāgrat stambhādipratyayavaditi.*

19. *"Atha rathān rathayogān pathaḥsṛjate iti", na ca "na tatra rathā na rathayogā na panthāno bhavanti" iti virodhādupacaritā .rthā sṛjata iti śrutirvyākhyeyā.*

20. *Sṛjata iti hi śruterbahu śruti saṁvādāt pramānāṇtara saṁvādā cca balīyastvena tadnuguṇatayā 'na tatra rathā' iti asyā bhā ktatvena vyākhyānāt.*

21. *Jāgradavasthā darśanayogya na santi na tu rathā nasantīti.*

22. *Prājñakartṛkatvāccāsya pārmārthikatvam viyadādisargavạt.*

23. Na ca-jīvakartṛkatvānna prājña*kartṛkatvam iti-sāmpratam; 'anyatra dharmād anyatra adharmāt' iti prājñasya eva prakṛtatvat.*

24. *Jivakartṛkatve'pi ca prājñād abhedena jivasya prājñatvāt.*

25. *Api ca jāgratpratyaya saṁvādavanto'pi svapna pratyayaḥ keciddṛśyante.*

26. *Tadyathā svapne suklāmbaradharaḥ śuklamālyanulepano .....narapatistvạm mānayiṣyatīti. Sa ca jagrattathā ātmano mā nanamanubhūya svapnapratyayam satyam abhimanyate.*

27. *Tasmāt sandhye pāramārthikī sṛṣṭiḥ*

28. *Māyāmātram tu kārtsnyena anabhivyaktasvarūpatvāt.*

29. *Na tāvat kṣīrasyeva dadhi rajatasya pariṇāmaḥ śuktiḥ sambhavati.*

30. *Na hi jātu Īśvaragṛhe cirasthitānyapi rajatabhājanāni śuktibhāvamanubhavanti dṛśyante.*

31. Na ca itarasya rajatānubhava samye'nyo 'nākulendriyo na tasya suktibhāvam anubhavati pratyeti ca.

32. *Na ca-ubhayarūpam vastu sāmagrībhedāt tu kadācid asyatoyabhāvo' nubhūyate kadācinmarīciteti sāmpratam.*

33. *Pārmārthike hi asya toyabhāve tat sādhyamudanyopaśamanalakṣaṇāmapi arthakriyām kuryānmrīcisādhyāmapi rūpaprakāśa lakṣaṇām.*

34. *Na marīcibhiḥ kasyacittṛṣṇaja udanyopaśāmyati, na ca toyamevam dvividhamudanyopasamanam atadupaśamanamiti yuktam, tadarthakriyākāritva vyāptam toyatvam matrayā pi tāmkurvattoyameva na syat.*

35. *Asamarthavidhāpāti toyametaditi manvāno na tṛṣṇayāpi marīcitoyam abhidhāvet yathā marīcīn anudhāvan. Athāśaktam śaktamabhimanyamāno' bhidhāvati. Kimaparāddham marīciṣu toyaviparyāsena sarvajanīnena?*

36. *Yattamatilaṅghya viparyāsāntaram kalpate.*

37. *Na ca kṣīradadhipratyayavadvā ācāryamātula brāhmaṇa pratyayavadvā toyamarīcivijñāne samuccitāvagāhinī; svānubhavāt paraspara viruddhayorbādhybādhakabhāva avabhāsanāt.*

38. *Tatrāpi rajatajñānam pūrvam utpannam bādhyamuttaram tu bādhakam śuktijñānam* prāptipūrvakatvāt pratiṣedhasya.

39. *Rajatajñānāt prākprāpakābhāvena śukteraprāptāyāḥ pratiṣedhāsaṁbhavāt pūrvajñāna prāptam tu rajatam śuktijñānamapabādhitum arhati. Tad apabādātmakam ca svānubhavād avasiyate.*

40. *Yathāhuḥ- 'āgāmitvād abādhitvāparam pūrvam hi jāyate, pūrvam punarabādhitvā param notpadyate kvacit'.*

41. *Na ca - Vartamāna rajatāvabhāsijñānam bhavisyattām asya agocarayan na bhaviṣyatā svasamayavartinīm śuktim*

gocarayatā pratyayena bādhyate, kālabhedena virodhābhāvā diti - yuktam.

42. *Mā nāmāsya jñāsītpratyakṣam bhavisyattām tatpṛṣṭhabhāvi tvanumānam upakārabhāvahetumivāsati vināśapratyayopanipāte sthemānam ākalayati.*

43. *Asati vināśapratyayopanipāte, rajatamidam sthiram rajatatvā d anubhūtapratyabhijñātarajatavat.*

44. *Tathā ca rajatagocaram pratyakṣam vastutaḥ sthirameva rajatam gocarayet. Tathāca bhaviṣyacchuktikājñānakālam rajatam vyāpnuyāditi virodhācchuktijñnena bādhyate.*

45. *Yathāhuḥ - 'rajatam gṛhyamāṇam hi cirasthāyīti gṛhyate, bhaviṣyacchuktikā-jñānakālam vyāpnoti tena tat' iti.*

46. *Pratyakṣena cirasthāyīṭi gṛhyata iti kecid-vyācakṣate. Tad ayuktam; yadi cirasthāyitvam yogyatā, na sā pratyakṣagocaraḥ śakteratīndriyatvat.*

47. *Atha kālāntara vyāpitvam, tad api ayuktam; kālāntarena bhaviṣyatendriyasya saṁprayogāt tad upahitasīmno vyāpitvasya atīndṛiyatvāt.*

48. *Na ca pratyabhijñāpratyayavad atrāsti saṁskāraḥ sahakārī, yena avartamānam api ākalayet. Tasmād atyantābhyā savaśena pratyakṣānantaram śīghratarotpanna vinaśyad avasthānumānasahita pratyakṣābhiprāyameva cirasthāyīti gṛhyata iti mantavyam.*

49. *Ata evaitat śukṣmataram kāla vyavadhānam avivecayantaḥ saugatāḥ prāhuḥ dvividho hi viṣaya pratyakṣasya grāhyaśca adhyavaseyaśca. Grāhyakṣaṇa ekaḥ svalakṣano' dhyavaseyaśca santāna iti.*

50. *Etena svapnapratyayo mithyātvena vyākhyātaḥ*

51. *Yattu satyam svapandarśanam uktam tatrāpyākhyātrā brā hmaṇāyanenākhyāte saṁvādābhāvād. Priyavratasya ākhyā na saṃvādastu kākatālīyo na svapnajñānam pramāṇayitumarhati tādṛśasyaiva bahulam visaṁvāda darśanāt.*

52. *Darśitaśca visaṁvādo bhāṣyakṛtā kārtsnyena anabhivyaktim vivṛṇvatā. Rajanīsamay'pi hi Bhāratādvarṣāntare ketumā ladau vāsaro bhavatiti Bhārate varsa ityuktam.*

53. *Darśanam sūcakam tacca svarūpeṇ sat, asattu dṛśyam.*

54. *Prājñavyāpāratvena pāramārthikatvānumānam pratyakṣeṇa bādhakapratyayena virudhyamānam na ātmānam labhata iti bhāvaḥ.*

THE ANALYSIS OF DREAM IN VIŚIṢTĀDVAITA:

The propounder of the *'Viśiṣṭādvaita'* school of Philosophy, Rā mānujācārya commented upon the B.Ss.* His commentary is known by the name of *Śrībhāṣya'*(Śrī.bhā). The *Bṛ. Upa.* says that in dreamstate there is creation. In order to corroborate this statement this *Upaniṣad* cites verse No. 4.3.10.[1] The meaning of this verse is 'There are no chariots, no animals to be yoked to them, no roads are there, but He creates the chariots, the animals and the roads. There are no pleasures, delights etc. but He is the agent of the creation'. Here doubt arises: *'Kimiyam rathādi sṛṣṭir Jīvena eva kriyate, āhosvid Īśvareṇa?'* 'whether the creation in the dreamstate is by *jīva or Īśvara?*'

At this stage the *Purvapakṣīin* says that *jīva* is the creator of dreams. And in order to support this he quotes the following *śruti* sentence: '*Sṛjate sa hi kartā*' (*Bṛ. Upa.* 4. 3. 10). There it can be apprehended that *Jīva* himself is the seer of the dreams.[2]

This too, is supported by one *Kaṭha* recension. It is said there that *Jīva* is the creator of the desired objects in dream.[3] They quote corroborative sentence from *Śruti 'Ya eṣu Supteṣu jāgarti kāmam kāmam puruṣo nirmimāṇaḥ' (Kaṭha.* 5.8). The meaning of this sentence is: 'He who remains awake when all are asleep, the *puruṣa* creates the various desired objects'. Here son etc. are pointed out by the word *kāma* but not disire.[4] Because, these are fit to be desired. To support this they cite supportive sentences from the *Śruti.*

'*Sarvān kāmām chandataḥ prārthayasva! (Kaṭha* 1.25)

'*Śatāyuṣaḥ putrapautrān Vṛṇisva' (Kaṭha.* 1.26)

So son etc. are the desired objects as per the context. Therefore, *Jīva* creates chariots etc. in dream.[5]

Jīva has '*Satyasaṁkalpatva*', it is known from the utterance of the Prajāpati.[6]

And hence, even in the absence of the materials creation is possible.[7]

Now the *Siddhāntin* will try to establish his view by refuting the views, stated above by the *Purvapakṣin*. He says in dream the creation of the objects like chariot ponds etc. are mere *māyā*, created by the *Paramapuruṣa*; this is what it means.[8]

Here the word *māyā denotes wonder as the meaning.*[9] *Since, the same 'word (māyā)* has occurred in the same sense in the *Rāmā yaṇa.*

'*Janakasya kulejātā devamāyā iva nirmātā!*' (*Rā. Bā.* 1. 27)

The meaning of this sentence is 'Born in the family of Janaka, created as the wonderful creation of the gods.'

'*Na tatra rathā, na rathayogā, na panthānaḥ*' - this *Śruti* sentence also conveys the meaning that all these objects were there but not fit to be experienced by a *puruṣa*[10] (who has little *Jñānaiśvarya* in comparison to *Paramapuruṣa*). Now, he creates chariots, paths by mere wishes. Being produced in him at that particular moment and these sort of momentary things are experienced by the dreamer in the dream-state for the time being. *Śruti* also says about the wonderful nature of these things itself.[11] Such wonderful creation is possible only on the part of the *Paramapuruṣa*, who has *satyasaṁkalpa* but not by *puruṣa*.[12] Because, although the *Jīva* is endowed with *satyasaṁkalpa* still the nature of *Jīva* is not manifested with its totality in the worldly state and hence, that type of wonderful creation is quite impossible in the case of the *Jīva*.[13] To support this view the *siddhāntin* quotes a corroborative evidence from *Śruti* '*Kāmam kāmam puruṣo nirmimāṇaḥ*' (*Kaṭha* 5.8.). Here he wants to say that *Paramapuruṣa* is the creator of all these desired objects and in order to corroborate the wonderful nature of *Paramapuruṣa* the *siddhāntin* cites the following *Śruti* sentences.

'Ya eṣu supteṣu jāgarti'.

'Tadeva śukram tad Brahma tad eva amṛtam ucyate'.

'Tasmin lokāḥśritāḥsarve tad

unātyeti kaścana'. (Kaṭha 5.8.)

From the beginning and concluding sentences of this verse we know the uncommon and extraordinary nature of the *Paramapuruṣa*. And that too, '*Atha veśāntān puṣkariṇiḥsravantiḥ sṛjate, sa hi kartā' (Bṛ Upa.*4.3.10) this śruti conveys the same sense as *Paramapuruṣa* alone can be the creator.[14] Now, the question is raised if it is accepted that *jīva* is natural because of the destruction of all sins, which were with him, then why won't he be able to manifest himself or his inner qualities? Sūtrakāra replies in the form of the *Sūtra* - *'Parābhidhyānāt, tu tirohitam tato hi asya bandha viparyayau'. Bhāṣyakāra-* states due to the desire of *Paramapuruṣa* the natural form of this *Jīva* is concealed.[15] Since the Jīva has committed so many mistakes in his series of beginningless *karman*, the *Paramapuruṣa* has concealed the natural auspicious form of the *Jīva* as punishment.[16] This very fact is corroborated by the following *Śrutipramāṇa:*

'Yadā hi eva eṣa etasmin adṛsye, 'nātmye' nirukte

'nilayane' bhayam pratiṣṭhām vindate, atha so'bhayam

gato bhavati. Yadā hi eva eṣa etasmin udaram

antaram kurute. Atha tasya bhāyam bhavati'. (Tai. Upa. 2.7.1)

'Eṣa hi eva ānandayāti' (Tai Upa. 2.7.1)

'Bhīṣāsmādvātaḥpavate' (Tai. Upa. 2.8.1)

So the bondage and solvation of the *Jīva* is dependent upon the wish of the *Paramapuruṣa* says the *Śruti*.

The concealment of the qualities of the *Jīva* is the effect of the attachment of the body or the association with the subtle non-sentient power.[17] At the time of creation qualities of the being exist due to the connection with the non-sentient entity, in the body form and at the time of destruction these hidden qualities remained with him because of the association with the extremely subtle non-sentient entity which is incapable of bifurcation into name and form.[18] Since the very nature of *Jīva* is not manifested in dream and hence, *Jīva* is not able to create chariots etc. by his mere desire.[19]

As the *Kaṭhopaniṣad says 'Tasmin lokāḥśritāḥsarve tadunātyeti kaścana.'* (*Kaṭha.* 5.8). The meaning is 'When all are asleep being awakened and being refuge of all the world etc.'-these are really possible only on the part of *Paramapuruṣa* and never on the part of *Jīva*.[20] Therefore, the *Paramapuruṣa* creates objects for the *Jīvas* in accordance with his meagre *karman*, whose longevity is of very shorter period of time, can be experienced by that particular *Jīva* only.[21]

And hence, the objects of the dream knowledge are not presupposed by the *Jīva saṁkalpa*.[22] Because, from *Śruti* we know that dream is indicative of future success or failure.[23]

The *Chāndyogyopaniṣad* says 'when a person sees a woman in dream, that indicates prosperity, but on the contrary if he sees a black man with black teeth, it denotes the earlier death of the dreamer caused by the dreamt-event.'[24]

So all these statements cited by the *siddhāntin* go to prove that the entities which appear in dream are indicative of future events. Those who are expert in chapters dealing with dream, they say that dreams are the indication of either auspicious or inasupicious.[25] The indicativeness is not possible from one's desire.[26] Therefore, an inauspicious thing which is undesirable, *Jīva* will never create, rather he will create all the while dreams which are indicative of something prosperous and auspicious.[27] But our general experience regarding dream tells us that exclusively we may not have auspicious dream. So authorisation cannot be given to the

Jīva. And hence, creation of the entities in dream are possible only by Īśvara and not by *Jīva*.[28]

NOTES AND REFERENCES

* Vide the *Srī.bhā.* on *B. Ss.* 3.2.1-6 as follows.

1. *'Na tatra rathā na rathayogā na panthāno bhavanti atha rathā n rathayogān pathaḥ sṛjate. Na tatrānanda mudaḥ pramudo bhavanti atha ānandān mudaḥpramudaḥsṛjate,..... Sa hi kartā.'* (*Bṛ. Upa.* 4.3.10)
2. *Svapnadṛgjīva eva tatra pratiyate.*
3. *Kim ca enam jīvam svapne kāmānām nirmātāram eke śā khino 'dhiyate?*
4. *Putrādayaśca tatra kāmyamānatayā kāmaśabdena nirdiśyante, na icchāmātram.*
5. *Ato rathādin jīvaḥsvapne sṛjati*
6. *Jivasya ca satyasaṁkalpatvam prajāpativākye śrutam.*
7. *Ata upakaraṇādi abhāve' pi sṛṣṭir upapadyate.*
8. *Svapne rathapuṣkariṇyādi arthajātam māyāmatram paramapuruṣa sṛṣṭam ityarthaḥ*
9. *Māyā śabdo hi āścaryavācī.*
10. *'Na tatra rathā na rathayogā na panthānaḥ' - sakaletara puruṣa anubhāvyatayā na bhavanti ityartha.*
11. *'Atha rathān rathayogān pathaḥ sṛjate' - svapnadṛg anubhā vyatayā tatkālamātra avasānān sṛjato iti āścarya rupatvam eva āha.*
12. *Evaṁvidha āścaryarūpa sṛṣṭiḥ satyasaṁkalpasya Paramapuruṣasya eva upapadyate na jīvasya.*
13. *Tasya satyasaṁkalpatvādi yuktasyāpi saṁsāradaśāyām kā rtsnyena anabhivyakta svarūpatvam na jīvaṣya tathāvidha ā ścarya sṛṣṭir upapadyate.*
14. *Iti upakrama upasaṁhārayoḥ Paramapuruṣa asādhāraṇasvabhāva pratiteḥ*

15. *Paramapuruṣa saṃkalpāt, asya jīvasya svāvhāvikam rupam tirohitam*
16. *Anādi karma paramparaya kṛta aparādhasya hi asya svābhā vikam kalyāṇarūpam Paramapuruṣaḥ tirodhāpayati.*
17. *So'pi tirobhāvo'pi dehayogādvārena vā bhavati, sukṣma acicchaktiyogād vāreṇa vā.*
18. *Sṛṣṭikāle dehāvasthā ena acidvastunā saṁyogād bhavati, pralayakāle nāmarupa vibhāga anarhāti sūkṣma acidvastuyo-gād.*
19. *Ato 'nabhivyakta svarūpatvāt svapne jīvo na rathādin saṁkalpamātreṇa sraṣṭum śaknoti.*
20. *Iti sarveṣu supteṣu jāgaraṇam sarvalokāśrayatvam ityādayoḥ hi Paramapuruṣasya eva saṁbhavanti.*
21. *Ataḥjīvānām alpālpa Karman anuguṇaphala anubhavārtham tāvanmātrakāla avasānām tadeka anubhāvyān arthān utpā dayati.*
22. *Itaśca svāpnā arthāḥ na jivasaṁkalpapūrvakāḥ*
23. *Yataḥsvapno 'bhyudayānabhyudayayoḥ sūcakaśca śruterava-gamyate.*
24. *'Yadā karmasu kāmyeṣu striyam svapneṣu paśyati.* Samṛddhim tatra jānīyāt tasmin svapnanidarśane' (*Chā. Upa.* 5.2.8).
25. *Svapnādhyāyavidaśca svapnam śubha-aśubhayoḥ* sūcakam ā cakṣate.
26. Sūcakatvam ca svasaṁkalpāyāttasya na upapadyate.
27. *Tathā ca aśubhasya aniṣṭatvād śubhasya sūcakameva sṛṣṭā paśyet.*
28. *Ataḥ svapne sṛṣṭir Iśvareṇa eva kṛtā.*

Dream in Dvaitādvaita Philosophy:

Nimbārka is another commentator of the B.Ss. His commentary is known by the name of '*Vedānta-Pārijāta-Saurabha*'. He is the propounder of the '*Dvaitādvaita*' school of Philosophy.

There is no difference in between '*Viśiṣṭādvaita*' and '*Davaitā dvaita*' school of Philosophy with regard to the dream-knowledge. According to Nimbārka also *Paramapuruṣa* is the creator of the dream-entities and not the *Jīva*.[1]

1. Cf. *Vedānta-Pārijāta-Saurabha*, pp. 51-52.

ANALYSIS OF DREAM IN BHEDĀBHEDA SCHOOL OF PHILOSOPHY

According to Bhāskarācārya* dream is nothing but an illusion (*māyā*). Here, he wants to mean by *māyā-'arthaśunyapratyaya*' i.e. the knowledge void of object. To be more clear, dream-knowledges are mere experiences. They never correspond to real objects of the world. But this doesnot mean that they donot have any substratum. He holds the view that the very characteristic phenomena of dream-experiences are remembrance of the past images of the entities appeared in knowledge at different times and at different places.[1]

The earlier impressions of the entities congregate in mind and being whirled in *Nāḍis* (veins) appear in dream as remembrance. And either by good or bad deeds of the dreamer, he sometimes dreams pleasure and sometimes frightful scene.[2]

This creation is of *Jīva* and not of '*Īśvara, because of the appearance of the entities in the form of pleasure and pain in dream.*[3]

Īśvara is the creator of only eternal entities like sky etc.[4] Bhā skara holds that the awakened-state objects are only true in the ultimate sense. Because, the awakened-state entities have relevance of time, place, presence of the entities, contact of the sense-organs with the objects and the absence of contradiction discriminate the dream-state objects from the awakened-state. *Kā rtsnya* is the totality or bundle of factors involved in order to justify the validity or trueness of the objects appearing in knowledge.

Dream-entities do not corroborate the space-time context. And hence, dream knowledge is unreal[5] To be more exact, dream objects can never be treated on a par with objects of the awakened-state and therefore, dream-objects are not real.

NOTES & REFERENCES

* *Vide Bhāskarācārya's comm. on B.Ss.* 3.2. 1-6. as follows:

1. *Deśāntara-kālāntara-anubhūta-anusmaraṇāt.*
2. *Svapne pūrvapravṛtti arthabhavajanitavāsanāvāsitam manaḥ nāḍīṣu parivartamānam smṛtijñānahetur bhavati śubhā śubhakarma preritam modatrāsādi darśanāt*
3. *Jīvasya sa eṣa sṛṣṭi sukha duḥkha pratibhāsanād na Īśvarasya.*
4. *Īśvarasya tu yā sṛṣṭiḥ ākāśādiviṣayā sā paramārthā eva.*
5. *Deśaḥ kālo viṣaya sannidhir indriya vyāpārobādhābhāvaśca kārtsnyam tenābhivyakta svarūpatva abhāvāt svapnasya.*

Dream In Śuddhādvaita Philosophy:

The propounder of the '*Śuddhādvaita* Philosophy', Vallabhācā rya is one of the famous commentator of the B.Ss. His commentary is otherwise known by the name of '*Aṇubhāṣya*'. *(Aṇu. bhā).**

At the very outset of this chapter (i.e. *Sandhyadhikaraṇam* 3.2.1) he holds the view that the content of the dream-knowledge is unreal[1]. Since the dream-entities do not have any relevance of time, place, etc. And hence, these are not real but mere illusion.[2] In other words, the dream entities do not manifest themselves full-fledgedly. *Śruti* speaks of the creation of the dream-entities but never points out anything about its reality.[3] With reference to other creation the term *satyam* is invariably used to indicate or support the trueness of the creation.[4] To him dream-state is nothing but *mā yā*, being originated from the *Mahāmāyāvī*. (i.e. the god). So He himself is the origin and source of the creation.[5]

As the commentator says each and every dream indicates something either auspicious or inauspicious effect through its content. In short, dream is a prophet[6]. It reveals or indicates in a symbolic way. Sometimes dream plays the role of an instructor. Dreamer gets directed through his dream.[7] This is the sum and substance of his whole discussion. In a way, Vallabha follows Śaṅkara in other points of discussion in order to falsify the state of dream and the content of the dream-knowledge.

NOTES & REFERENCE

* See *Aṇu. bhā.* on B.Ss. 3.2. 1-6 as follows:

1. *Svapnasya mithyātvam pradarśayitum adhikaraṇārambha.*
2. Svapnasṛṣṭir māyāmātram, tatra hetu kārtsnyena anabhibyaktasvarupatvāt. Kṛtsnatvena yasya yādṛsam svarūpam deśakālavastusāpekṣam.
3. Śruti sṛṣṭim eva āha, 'Na tatra ratha na rathayogā... sṛjate' (Bṛ. Upa. 4.3.10) *ityādinā sṛṣṭiḥ āha.*
4. *"Aitadātmyamidam sarvam tat satyam" (Chā. Upa. 8.8.7) iti, "Tat satyam iti ācakṣate" (Tai. Brā. 6) ityādi śruti sahasrebhyo asya satyatvam pratīyate.*
5. *Svapnamātravihārastu Mahāmāyāvitvān māyayāpi sidhyati.*
6. *Śubhāśubhaphalasūcako bhavati svapnaḥ.*
7. *Kvacid* ājñāviśeṣadānam.

Dream in Dvaita Philosophy

The founder of the 'Dvaita' school of Philosophy is Madhvācārya who has putforth his view* precisely regarding the validity of creation in the dreamstate and the agentship of the creation.

According to him in dream-state there is creation. And this fact is also supported by the *Śruti*.[1] He says that the entities which appear in dream are nothing but the beginningless past experiences, accumulated in the mind of the *Jīva*. These assembled experiences only come up in the form of dream when *Parameś-vara* activates them.[2] In other words, *Jīva* is inert in dream-state. He has no function in the revival of the past experiences. *Parameśvara* is the only authority to get them actuated in the innate creative mind of the *Jīva.* [3]

The very characteristic of the dream phenomenon is the revival of the past impressions and this is the reason for which the dream-entities do not satisfy the stipulations of the place-time etc. exactly in the same way as the entities of the awakened-state fulfill those requirements in order to make them valid. Therefore, dreams are not caused by any means other than past impressions because, they are not manifested fully.[4] In dream-state external sense-organs are withdrawn to operate with regard to the outward world. So on the basis of the data, already available in the mind of the *Jīva*, mind functions and creates entities as per the wish of *Parameśvara.* Therefore, dreams are designated by the term 'manogatā saṁskārā'. Saṁskāras act as materials or the essential factors of dream production. In order to strengthen the agentness of *Parameśvara* as the creator of the entities in the dream-state *Bhāṣyakāra* has given another evidence. In the absence of other means, due to the indication of present and non-present entities in dream *Īśvara* alone can be thought of as the creator.[5] Due to the wish of *Parameśvara, Jīva* gets associated with bondage and the constant meditation on Him enable a person to get rid of bondage i.e. the attainment of liberation. So since bondage or liberation depends on the desire of God. And hence, he alone is the creator or dispellor of the dream events.[6].

NOTES AND REFERENCES

* Vide the *Bhāsya of B.S.s. 3.2. 1-6 by Madhvācārya, (Mā. bhā .) as follows:*

1. *Bṛ. Upa.* 4.3.10.
2. Anādi manogatān saṁskāran svecchāmātreṇa pradarśayati
3. *Manogatāṁśca saṁskārān svecchayā Parmeṣvaraḥ pradar-śayati Jīvāya sa svapna iti gīyate.*
4. *Anabhivyaktarūpatvād na anya sādhanajam bhavet.*

4. Anabhivyaktarūpatvād na anya sādhanajam bhavet.
5. Sādhanāntara abhāve' pi bhāvābhāva sūcakatvena Īśvaro darśayati
6. Svapnādibuddhikartā ca tiraskartā sa eva ca. Tadicchayā yato hi asya bandha-mokṣau pratiṣṭhitau.

III. 1. POSITION IN SĀṀKHYA-YOGA

Analysis of Dream in Sāṁkhya:

Maharṣi Kapil holds that dream is illusory by nature (i.e. unreal). Among the *Sāṁkhya-sūtras* we get only one reference of dream (svapna)! This sūtra is explained further by Vijñānabhikṣu in his *sāṁkhya-pravacana-bhāṣya* as follows:

He says that it is not possible to obtain the unified *puruṣārtha (ekaḥ puruṣārtha;* i.e. the unity of *dharma, artha, kāma and mokṣa)*, being mutually accompanied by the illusory *(māyika)* and non-illusory *(amāyika)* entities of the dream-state and the awakened- state because of their unreal and unsteady nature.[2] *Gauḍapādabhāṣya* and *Yuktidīpikā* also support the same view.[3] *Yuktidīpikā* again says that a dream-knowledge is perverse-remembrance. Because, a particular entity appears in various forms.[4] Sāṁkhyāḥ(the supporter of this system of Philosophy) like Vedāntins, especially the propounder of the theory of *māyāvāda* are of the opinion that dream is caused by *saṁskāra* and hence, it is *smṛti*[5]. Śaṁkara in his *Jayamaṅgalā* does not talk about the nature of dream. He simply points out how this knowledge is produced.[6] *Sāṁkhyakārikā, Maṭharavṛtti, Tattvaprabhā, Tattvakaumudī, Aniruddhavṛtti* etc. do not say anything about dream. Here, we find a difference between the Vedāntins and Sāṁkhyas though they are of the same opinion that dream-knowledge is produced by impression still according to the Vedāntins the entities of the awakened-state is false and at par with the dream-state. On the contrary, *Sāṁkhya-sūtra* (3/26) itself points out the *amāyika* (i.e. non-illusory) characteristics of the entities of the awakened-state.

Analysis of Dream in Yoga.

In the *Yogasūtra* of Patanjali we find only one occurrence of *svapna* (i.e. 1/38). This aphorism occurs in the *samādhipāda* of this treatise. The meaning of this aphorism is "The knowledge of the dream or sleep may be the object of study for the steadiness of mind."[1]

Tattvavaiśāradī (T.Vai) of Vācaspati Miśra further clarifies how this steadiness is acquired by mind after dream-vision. When a yogi in his dream-state being settled in a solitary spot of a forest, worships the image of Lord Maheśvara which appears as if coming out from the moon-disk, whose minor and major limbs appear as soft as lotus stalks and made up of precious moon-stone and encircled by garlands of *mālati* and *mallikā* flowers having sweet fragrance. After getting up, in highly pleasant mental state he remembers the same form being one with that and obtain the steadiness of mind.[2]

The *Vṛtti* of Bhoja defines what dream is? He says: when the outwardly oriented sense-organs *(bāhyendriya)* have stopped functioning or the five external sense-organs are inactive to function at that time only mentally there is a tendency to enjoy *(bhoktṛtva)* by *ātman* (soul), that is called *svapna*. This is confined to *ātman* only.[3] *Yogamañjarī* also defines dream as 'when all sorts of external sensory-function is abandoned and the mind alone acts internally that is *svapna*'.[4] Now, the question arises: what short of knowledge is this? The answer is being given by the *Bhāṣyakāra* Vyāsa that this is a type of remembrance. He explains further by saying that *smṛti* is of two types: in one case, a phenomenon, which is to be remembered by mind only *(bhāvitasmartavyā)* and in the other case the vice-versa, then we say that the earlier effort of mind is of the dream-state and the next one is of the awakened-state.[5]

But Vācaspati Miśra refutes this stand by saying that since the dream knowledge satisfies the definition of *viparyaya* it can no longer be called *smṛti* Because of the resemblance with *smṛti* we may term this knowledge as *smṛti*.[6]

Bālarāmodāsin in his commentary supports the view of Vā caspati. To deny the *smṛtitva* of dream-knowledge he forwards arguments as follows;

He says if one accepts dream-knowledge as *smṛti* (remembrance) then the form of sentence or expression will never occur in dream 'this horse' or after awakening 'I saw a king'. Because this type of form never occurs in remembrance *(smṛti). Smṛti* knowledge assumes the form like 'that horse' or 'I remembered a king'. So it is to be held that dream-knowledge is quite different from *smṛti*. In order to corroborate his argument he quotes a *śruti* '*Neyam smṛtirapi tu viparyaya*.[7] Vijñānabhikṣu tries to interprete it in other way by taking '*bhāvitasmartavya*' as the indicative of future. According to him one should not hold that dream-knowledge cannot be categorized as *smṛti* on the ground that this knowledge does not fulfil the criteria of *smṛti* namely, reminding the events seen in the past, sometimes and produced by *saṁskāra*. But as a matter of fact, dream-knowledge partially satisfies both the criteria. So it should be treated as *smṛti*. [8]

Tattvavaiśāradī again points out that the container or locus of the dream-knowledge is *citta (svapnajñā*nālambanacittam).[9] On the Other hand, Vijñānābhikṣu holds the view that in the knowledge of the worldly objects *citta* has the same status as that of the dream-state.[10] So it seems he (Vijñānabhikṣu) perhaps does not want to make any distinction of mind in explaining the knowledge of both the states.

NOTES AND REFERENCES

1. *Svapnajāgarābhyām iva....... (Sāṁ. sū. 3.26)*
2. *Māyika amāyikābhyām svapnajāgarapadārthābhyām anyo'nya sahakāribhāvena ekaḥ purusārtho na saṁbhavati. Mā yikatvam ca asatyatvam, asthiratvam, iti. Jāgratpadārthastu..... asthiratvena asatyatvād. (Bhā.p. 132)*

3. *Svapna indrajāla sadṛsam iti (Gau. Bhā. p. 113). Mṛgatṛśṇikā-svapnaviṣayairasadbhiḥ...viparitadarśana-prasaṁgaḥ (Yuk. pp. 164)*
4. *Svapne ca ekamūrtipatitānām go-puruṣa-aśva-rāsava.... darśaṇam smaraṇe viparyayeṇa dṛṣṭam. (Yuk. p. 165)*
5. *Sāṁkhyāḥ māyāvādivedāntinaśca saṁskāramātrajanyaḥ .... svapnaḥ iti āhuḥ (Nyā. Ko. p. 1053)*
6. *Yat svapnadarśanam tad indriya vyatireki, nidrā upaplutatvād indriyānām. (Jaya. p. 70)*

1. *Svapnanidrājñānālambanam vā* (Yoga. sū 1/38).
2. *Yadā khalu ayam svapne viviktavanasanniveśavartinīm-utkīrnām iva candramandalāt komalamṛnālaśakalānukā ribhir aṅgapratyaṅgair upetām abhijāta candrakānta-maṇimayīm atisurabhimālatī mallikā malāhārinīm mano-harām Bhagavato Maheśvarasya pratimām ārādhayan eva prabuddhaḥprasannamanāstadā tāmeva svapnajñānāvalam-banībhūtām anucintya-yatastasya tad ekākārmanaḥ tatraiva cittam sthitipadam labhate. (T. Vai. on Sū. 1/38)*
3. *Partyastamitavāhya indriyavṛttermanomātreṇaiva yatra bhoktṛtvamātmanaḥ sa svapna. (Vṛtti on sū 1/38)*
4. *Bāhyasakalavṛtti parityāgena cetaso' bhyantaravāhitā svapna iti yogamañjarī* (Kārikā. 1/25).
5. Grāhyākārapūrvā smṛtiḥ, sā ca dvayī-bhāvitasmartavyā ca abhāvitasmartavyā ca, svapne bhāvitasmartavyā, jāgrat samaye tu abhāvitasmartavyā iti (V. Bhā. on Sū 1/11).
6. Neyam smṛtirapi tu viparyayaḥ, tallakśaṇopapannatvāt, smṛtyābhāsatayā tu smṛtirukta.... (T. Vai. on sū 1/11)
7. Mishra, Umesh, "Dream Theory in Indian Thought" ..pp 281-82.
8. Svapnadarśanam eva hi bhāvyarthasūcakatayā śāstre siddham...., nanu svapne pūrvadṛstatvāsmaraṇāt saṁskāramā trajanyatva abhāvācca katham smṛtitvam iti cet, na-

aṁśatastadubhayarūpatvasya svapnajñāneśu api sattvāt tādṛsasya svapnāṁśasya iva atra upanyāsād iti. (Vār on sū. 1/11)

9. Svapnajñānālambanam cittam (Yo. Ko. pp. 108).
10. Svapṇajñānam....tad ālambakam cittam prapancajñāne svapnadṛṣṭimaccittam iti yāvat (Vār. p. 104).

III. 2 POSITION IN MĪMĀṀSĀ

Śabara on Dream-knowledge:

Mīmāṁsakas are of the opinion that a real-sense-perception involves three factors namely, the mind, sense-organ and the object of knowledge. The real contact of these three things they have termed as *satsaṁprayoga*. In the absence of any one of these three, false knowledge arises.

Now, the Buddhists start arguing to deny the objective reality which is one of the factors of real perception by an inferential syllogism as follows:* *Pratijña* (Proposition): Knowledges are objectless. *Hetu* (Reason): It is a knowledge. *Udāharaṇa* (Example); Like the dream-knowledge (The very nature of dream-knowledge is, it is a knowledge without corresponding external object). *Upanaya* (corroboration): In the awakened state same type of knowledge arises. e.g. a pillar or a wall.

Nigamana (conclusion): So this knowledge (i.e. the knowledge of the awakened state) is also objectless,.[1]

Śabara says in reply that the knowledge of a pillar in the awakened-state is confirmed. How can it be a contradictory knowledge?[2] Buddhists' say in the dream-state too the knowledge is certain as long as the person dreams. In other words, the knowledge of dream is also real till the person gets up. So there should not be any difference between the two knowledges viz. the knowledge of the awakened state and that of the dream-state. They are said to be one and the same.[3] Śabara denies the Buddhists stand by pointing out that in dream perverse-knowledge takes place. On the contrary, that never arises during the awakening-state.[4]

Buddhists again say from the analogical point of view the awakened state knowledge can also be termed as perverse.[5]

Now Śabara comes to refute the stand of the Buddhists as follows:

If the knowledge of dream is false since it is a knowledge, then on the same ground the knowledge of the awakened-state will be false.[6]

Since, knowledge is the *hetu* to make both the knowledges on a par hence, on the basis of that you cannot claim that the knowledge of dream is unreal—says Śabara.[7] According to him *svapnapratyaya* is false because it gets contradicted in the awakened-state.[8]

Again Buddhists raise question: how could you know this fact?[9] Śabara says in sleep-state mind becomes weak and *nidrā* (sleep) causes *mithyābhāva* (i.e. falsity). A knowledge, which arises before *svapna* and after *svapna* but never in the *suṣupti* state cannot be false. *Suṣupti* state is called as unconscious-state *(acetana)*. The absence of knowledge is there.[10] From all these we may conclude that the knowledge of the awakened-state is not false.[11] Because, in the awakened state *nidrābhāva* is there. Further, the Buddhists say that as mind is overpowered in *nidra*, which is *karaṇadoṣa* also takes place in Jāgrat.[12] Śabara says if karaṇadoṣa is there that can be known. But while dreaming that is not possible to detect the *karaṇadoṣa* and this is the difference between the two states. Only after getting up from dream one realises that his mind was affected by sleep.[13] Thus, the object of a dream-knowledge is not true but false.

Analysis of Dream in Prabhākara School of Pūrva-mīmāṁsā

Prabhākara Miśra, in his *Bṛhati, (Bṛ)** points out the Buddhists' idealism that all knowledges are without real objects like the knowledges of dreams. When this is the fact, how to justify the definition of perception?[1]

A real-perception requires the contact of a real object and the sense-organ then how can you say that all knowledges are without object? We have known so far the very nature of dream-knowledge that it is a knowledge without object.[2] But it is never the case with the knowledge of silver after seeing a conch. Because, this is *smṛtijñāna* (remembered knowledge).[3] The glittering colour of conch-shell being delimited by eyes prompts to remember silver, since it has similar glittering character.[4]

In the case of the dream-knowledge remembrance doesnot arise about other object since it cannot accept external object.[5] Because the resemblance of an entity makes us remember about the otherone which possesses that quality. This is only possible in the awakened-state knowledge, e.g. *śuktirajatajñāna*, but not in the knowledge of the dream-state since there is no object.[6] Therefore, this is to be accepted that the dream-knowledge is caused by *vāsanā* (impression).[7]

Now, the Opponent asks if you accept impression alone is the cause which gives rise to dream then the brevity of imagination will arise because of its non-applicability to the similar object which are non-existent in dream.[8] Thus, the knowledge of wall is caused by the impression and not by the object wall this type of contingency will arise.[9]

In order to remove this contingency the Proponent replies: A cause is especially meant for the achievement of the *kārya* (the effect) but never for the destruction.[10] In dream-knowledge the externally manifested objects also appear which is not possible without the existence of the object in the external-world.[11] Again, without something which cannot come into existence that something is the cause of that.[12] Thus, it is proper to conceive *artha* (object) as cause of the dream-knowledge.[13] *Nirālambanatā* i.e. the objectlessness of the knowledge is not known because of *pratyakṣa* (i.e. the perceptual knowledge).[14] Therefore, the knowledge is produced by eyes and not by *Vāsanā*. From all these we may deduce that a knowledge of dream is not false after awakening.[15]

It is not wise to conceive something false as the cause of a knowledge-says the Opponent.[16] Now, the Proponent encounters by saying that where there is no cause even a false-knowledge does not arise.[17] The Opponent again says what you say that is true but that cause does not facilitate to cognise that knowledge.[18] The Proponent answers that due to its presence the state of being a false-knowledge should not arise.[19] Thus, *Vyāmoha* (the void of object) causes *mithyāpratyaya* (false-knowledge). And these *vyāmohas* are caused by the worldly impressions. Therefore, impressions *(vā sanās)* cause this type of *mithyāpratyaya* — stated by the *tattvavidas* (those who have known the essence of knowledge).[20]

In the case of the *smṛtijñāna* the structure of knowledge is 'I remember' and hence *smṛtijñānas* are void of knowledges. And this type of eroded knowledge (i.e. the *smṛti)* cannot act as a prompting factor of a knowledge[21]. Further, it is also possible that dreams are caused by either thought *(cintā)* or *adṛṣṭa* (fortune). Because, in dream sometimes we have the knowledge of pleasure and pain. And these are caused by *adṛṣṭa*[22]. Therefore, it is obtained that the *svapnajñāna*, produced by *adṛṣṭa* is caused by some thought *(kiṁcitcintādihetukam)* and will be on par with the knowledge of *śukti* etc. of the awakened state.[23]

So in other words, the knowledge of the dream-state and that of the awakened-state is one and the same.

Pramoṣa (erosion) causes falsity in dream.[24] To be more clear, when sense-organs do not function with efficiency and mind gets overpowered then only erosion of knowledge produces falsity in dream. This seems to be the stand of Prabhākara Mīmāṁsaka regarding the objective reality of dream-knowledge.

Analysis of Dream in the Bhāṭṭa school of Pūrva-mīmāṁsā:

In the *Nirālambanavāda of Ślokavārtika* of Kumārilabhaṭṭa Buddhist Idealists, deny the external objective reality by classifying the reality into two heads namely, the true reality *(Paramārtha-satya)* and the false-reality *(samvṛtisatya)*. External reality comes under later head. And under this criterion the authoritativeness of *vidhi, mantra, arthavāda* etc. get falsified. In order to nullify the external reality with which we behave in our day-to-day life, they have adopted an inferential syllogism.

The inferential syllogism, supra, pp. 57. In course of argument the proponent has tried to point out various kind of faults in their proposed syllogism as follows:

The proponent says that when there are two kinds of false knowledges namely, the *karaṇadoṣajñāna* (i.e. the knowledge produced by the disease-stricken organs) and the *bādhaka-jñāna* (i.e. the contradictory-knowledge), how do you propose all knowledges are false?

Again, by saying 'all' you have already included dream-knowledge in that category so there is no such knowledge which can be cited as an instance. If you (Idealist) hold that all cognitions are absolutely devoid of substratum then the qualifier of your proposition will be devoid of base and there will be no such example to corroborate the fact. Because, in dream cognised objects sometimes become true in the awakened-state says the proponent. The proponent gives a counter inferential syllogism to reject the syllogism of the opponent and to establish the external objective reality. The syllogism is like this. Proposition: cognitions have real substratum in external world.

Because, it is a notion free from contradiction. e.g. Like the notion of the falsity of the dream-cognition. The proponent further says if you oppose that the notion of the falsity of the dream-cognition is not true then dream cognition will never be unreal to you. And it can never be cited as an example as you have cited in your syllogism.

It is also not proper to reject a knowledge which is unreal without examination. By this way the awakened-state knowledge too will be rejected like dream-knowledge. A knowledge which is contradicted by a subsequent knowledge that alone can be rejected otherwise not. And in the case of the awakened-state knowledge too if this type of contradictory-knowledge arises that will be rejected by that knowledge which has arisen later.[1]

There is a discussion in the *Nirālambanavāda* of *Śāstradīpikā* of Parthasarathi Miśra about the denial of the objective reality of the world by the nihilists.

There, the opponent tries to establish his stand by saying that knowledge terminates in itself by showing the object because of beginningless impressions. So its outward appearance is false. And that can be known by means of inference. The inferential syllogism, taken up by the opponent to deny the external reality is as follows:

Proposition *(Pratiñja)*: Though the pillar is a self-terminated object still its outward existence makes it false.

Reason *(Hetu)*: Because, it is a knowledge.

Example *(Udāharana)* (a): The knowledge of a dream entity is unreal externally because outwordly existent entity nullify its reality. (b) The knowledge of the silver on conch is also like that.

Corroboration *(Upanaya)*: The knowledge of the awakened state is also like that.

Conclusion *(Nigamana)*: Hence, the awakened state knowledge is false.

Further, the opponent says the knowledge of dream is obtained in the absence of external entities and it is also not possible for those entities to appear in dream belong to different place and different time due to their closeness *(saṁnihitadeśakālatayā)*. But mere a chance, which is not possible that also appears in dream. e.g. the head of a person is being cut off by himself. So it is evident that dream-knowledge is self-cognised and it cognises itself like outside. Thus, due to that similarity the knowledges of the awakened-state also terminate in itself and hence this is false.

Now, the proponent comes to refute the stand of the opponent on proper ground. He points out that the view held by the opponent that the dream-knowledge has self-terminated object and it cognises itself in the form of *viṣaya* is not correct. Because, the dream-knowledge not only cognises self-terminated object *(svā ṁśāvalambanā)* but also cognises object existing outside in their various forms.

If you hold that the dream-knowledge cognises objects existing only inside. This also doesnot hold true. Because, the knowledge of blue which has no form cannot be cognised itself. But we find the external usages with form like 'this is blue', 'this is yellow' etc. And this type of expression refers to their appearance in knowledge with form which arises out of contact between the object and the eyes. So these are perceptual knowledges and hence, cannot be denied by means of inference.

Again, if it is a fact that the knowledge cognises itself then due to its self-cognisibility the knowledge will be 'I am blue' (aham nī laḥ).

As a matter of fact, *pratyakṣa* presents all those entities outside and denies the origination of inference, which is very much apt to deny the external reality.

The dream-knowledge cannot refer external entities as its substratum. Because, the knowledge of the awakened-state prohibits the external reality of dream-entities. So in dream-state alone self-cognisibility is possible but not in the awakened-state knowledge. In the awakened-state knowledge there will be no *bādhaka* (contradictor) other man *anumāna* (inference). And *amnumāna* can no longer contradict *pratyakṣa* because, *anumāna* is based upon *pratyakṣa*. So the knowledge of the entities in the awakened-state would never be false and in comparison to the awakened-state knowledge dream-knowledge is false.[1]

NOTES & REFERENCES

*See the commt. (Bāsya) of Śabara (Śāb-bhā) on sū. No. 1.1.5.

1. *Nanu sarva eva nirālambanaḥ svapnavat pratyayaḥ Pratyayasya hi nirālambanatā-svabhāva upalakṣitaḥ svapne. Jāgrate'pi stambha iti vā kuḍya iti vā pratyaya eva bhavati tasmāt so' pi nirālambanaḥ*
2. *Ucyate. Stambha iti jāgrato buddhiḥ supariniścitā katham viparyasi vyaṁtīti?*
3. *Svapne api evam supariniścitā 'sītprākprabodhanād na tatra kaścid viśeṣa iti.*
4. *Na, svapne viparyayadarśanāt. Aviparyayād ca itarasmin.*
5. *Tatsāmānyādi itara atra api bhaviṣyatīti.*
6. *Yadi pratyayatvād svapna pratyayasya mithyābhāvaḥ jā gratpratyayasyāpi tathā bhavitum arhati.*
7. *Pratītistathābhāvasya hetuh, na sakyate pratyayatvād ayam anya iti vaktum.*
8. *Anyatastu svapnapratyayasya mithyābhavo viparyayād avagataḥ*
9. Kuta iti cet?
10. *Sanidrasya manaso daurvalyād nidrā mithyābhāvasya hetuḥ svapnādau svapnānte ca suṣuptasyābhāva eva. Acetayan eva hi suṣupta ityucyate.*
11. *Tasmād jāgrataḥ pratyayo na mithyeti.*
12. *Nanu jāgrato' pi karaṇadoṣa syāt.*
13. *Yadi syād avagamyet. Svapnadarśanakāle' pi na avagamyata iti cet. Tatra prabuddho hi avagacchati nidrākrāntam me mana āsīd iti.*

* Vide Bṛ of Prabhākara on su. 1.1.5 (p. 68–74 of Madras ed) as follows:

1. *Nanu sarva eva nirālambanaḥsvapnavat pratyayaḥ; kutastatsaṁprayuktatvam atatsaṁprajuktatvam vā, yena viśeṣeṇa pratyaksa, apratyakṣayor viśeṣa upalabyate?*
2. *Katham punaḥsarva eva nirālambanaḥpratyayaḥ? pratyayasya hi nirālambanatā svabhāva upalakṣitaḥ svapne.*
3. *Nanu śuktikāyām rajatajñānam........smṛtijñānamuktam.*
4. *Śuktikāyām yad bhāsvararūpam cakṣuṣā paricchinnam tad rajatasmṛter udbodhakam iti upapadyeta.*
5. *Svapnādiṣu punaḥ kasyacid agrahaṇād arthāntare smṛti udbodha parihāraḥ.*
6. *Sadṛśadarśanāt sadṛse 'rthāntare smṛter udbodhaḥ; svapne punaḥ kasyacid agrahaṇād ityuktam.*
7. *Tasmād vāsanānibandhanam eva idam jñānajālam iti pratipadyāmahe.*
8. *Tasmād vāsanā eva nimittam iti laghvī kalpanā; na arthāntarā śrayaṇam, avyāpteḥ*
9. *Ataḥ kuḍyādisu api jñānam vāsanā nimittam eva, na kuḍyā rthanimittam iti sthitiḥ.*
10. *Ucyate-kāryasiddhyartham hi kāraṇam kalpyate, na punaḥkā rya vināśāya.*
11. *Svapnādiṣu ca bahir avabhāsā saṁvit; sā ca bāhyam artham antareṇa na saṁbhavati.*
12. *Yena ca vinā yad na saṁbhavati, tat tasya kāraṇam.*
13. *Tasmād artha eva kāraṇam iti yuktam kalpyitum.*
14. *Nirālambanatā tu na eva saṁvedyate partyakṣa avabodhena.*
15. *Tasmād aksajam jñānam, na vāsanānimittam ityuktam. Nanu ca pratibuddhasya svapnopalabdham mithyā.*

16. *Na ca mithyābhāvasya kāraṇakalpanā.*
17. *Nanu ca akāraṇasya mithyāpratyayasya utpādo na ghatate.*
18. *Satyam, na tu avagati anuguṇam tat.*
19. *Tad anuguṇye hi mithyājñānatā* eva na syāt.
20. *Tasmād vyāmohahetavo mithyāpratyayāḥ vyāmohani bandhanāśca sāṁsārikyo vāsanāḥ. Ato vāsanā nibandhanam eva idam jñāna*jālam uditam tattvavidbhiḥ.
21. *Smrāmi iti jñānaśūnyāni smṛtijñānāni* etāni. Nanu smṛter udbodhakāraṇa asaṁbhavād.
22. *Svapnādau api hi cintādṛstādisaṁbhavāt, svapne' pi hi sukhaduḥkham anubhūyate; sukhaduḥkhahetuśca adṛṣṭam.*
23. *Ato 'dṛṣṭahetukam eva svapnādijñānam kincid cintādihetukam iti upapannam śuktikādi jñānatulyatvam svapnādijñānasya*
24. *"Anyato hi svapnapratyayasya mithyābhāvaḥ" iti pramoṣanimittatām darśyayati.*

1. *Ślokavārtika* of Kumārila Bhaṭṭa, Varanasi ed, 1978, cf. the gist of Śloka No. 1-3, 5, 18, 22-24, 49, 79, 80, 81, 87, 88.
1. *Cf. Miśra, Parthasarāthi, Śāstradīpikā, on sū. 1.1.5 (pp, 81-84 of Varanasi ed)*

III.3 POSITION IN NYĀYA-VAIŚEṢIKA

Analysis of Dream in the Nyāya-School:

The *Nyāya-sūtra* 4.2.31 presents and examines the Buddhist-Idealists' notion of means of acquiring knowledge *(Pramāṇā)* and the object of knowledge *(Prameya)*. According to them both are unreal because both are of the form of knowledge. To establish this they have taken the help of the knowledge of dream.[1]

Sūtra 4.2.34 tries to examine the nature of dream-knowledge. Here, Gautama says the dream-knowledge has the object like that of remembrance *(smṛti)* or longing *(saṁkalpa,* i.e. the desire for the obtainment of an entity apprehended earlier).[2]

The Bhāṣyakāra Vātsyāyana argues that as remembrance and longing have objects of knowledge which were apprehended earlier likewise dream-knowledge also has an object, experienced before. No one can deny this fact that the objects of remembrance or longing has to be cognised earlier. Same is the fact in the case of a dream-knowledge.[3]

This implies that the objects of dream-knowledges have to be real. In short, the knowledge acquired in the dreamstate must have a definite substratum in the awakened-state.

This is also supported by the fact that one who dreams during sleep, recollects and verifies after getting up from the dream saying 'such and such thing I saw in the dream'. Being influenced by the knowledge of the awakened state, the dreamer thinks that the object of the dream-knowledge is unreal.[4]

Proponent says if we do not draw any distinction between the two states namely the awakened-state and the dream-state then the arguments become meaningless. Those who do not want to maintain such distinction with reference to reality between both the states, for them the idea of means and the object is like the knowledge of dream. And the arguments putforth by them to establish *Pramāṇa* and *prameya* as false will have no meaning. Because, they reject the notion of a real objective counterpart of a wrong-knowledge.[5] A wrong-knowledge is always based upon a real object. e.g. the knowledge of a man on pillar which is not a man but which appears as a man has a real substratum. This can never be the case that one who has no knowledge of man will have the knowledge of a man. Likewise, the knowledge of dream is also based upon a real objective counterpart of the awakened-state.[6] And by the true-knowledge of an entity the wrong-apprehension gets negated but not the object.[7]

Vārtikakāra (Udyotakara) supports the same view as it is held by Gautama and Vātsyāyana. He says that the object of dream-knowledge is just like the objects of either *smṛti* or *saṁkalpa*. But not like any imaginary city or mirage-water. Because, there is no such proof to corroborate this fact.[8] Here, the knowledge of the objects which are non-existent cannot be cited as cause of that knowledge after dream.[9] Now, the question arises that after dream-state the objects of knowledge do not exist at all so what was the cause of that knowledge.[10] If we say that the cognition is the cause then the contingency arises as follows:[11]

Apart from consciousness the objects apprehended in the awakened-state are non-existent. So the acceptance of cognition as cause becomes like dream.[12]

The Proponent objects this by saying 'no'. Because, this example is as unproved as the probandum.[13] Someone asks again, whatever object we cognise in dream-state is not different from the consciousness then what is the reason of their being apart from consciousness.[14] The answer is given that after awakening they do not exist.[15]

The proponent asks: do you mean by this that after getting up from sleep which is not cognised is non-existent?[16] But that cannot be said because of the employment of your qualifying term i.e. those objects which are cognised after awakening are existent. The qualifier will be futile if we do not apprehend the things after coming back to the awakened state.[17] It implies that things do exist in the awakened state.

Further, he argues that if you (Idealists) think that the objects apprehended in the dream-state do not exist in the awakened state then on the basis of that ground how will you prove the existence of consciousness?[18] Again, the fact of non-apprehension in the awakened-state, which you have taken as the ground *(hetu)* for your denial has no capability to prove the allegation put forth by you.[19] Because, the apprehension implies the existence of the entity and the non-apprehension the contrary. So the non-apprehension can act as an efficient cause to contradict your proposition.[20]

According to you if only consciousness exists then you should also accept the fourfold division of that.[21] He who doesnot admit the fourfoldness of consciousness and accepts only what he perceives should be questioned to explain the differences of cognition which have been perceived by him. But as a matter of fact, there is no such cause either eternal or external which distinguishes one cognition from the other. So how can difference occur?[22] If one holds the view that the diversity of cognitions is like the diversity of dreams still it should be stated that due to the impressions of the real entities perceived and experienced during the tenure of life diversity takes place in dream-cognitions. So the diversity in dream is caused by the impressions of the past.[23] The difference of dream is due to the difference of impression of the real object. And it should be stated due to the difference between imagining and the imagined object because, they are not identical.[24]

So if at all in dream diversity arises that is because of impression and it has to correspond to some real object.

The dream-knowledges which reveal different entities like city, chariot etc. are if not verifiable unreal because they are at par with the erroneous knowledges of the awakened-state.[25]

He who doesnot want to accept the existence of anything beside 'consciousness', should explain the difference between the waking-state and the dream-state. According to them there is no real object of apprehension in the awakened-state also like the object of the dream-state. In short, to you both states are one and the same, then why such distinction namely, 'this is the dream state' and 'this is the awakened state?'[26]

Again, if you do not make any distinction then there will be no difference between merit and demerit. e.g. any sin committed in dream will not be attached to the person; same is the case in the awakened-state.[27]

The simple difference between these two states is, in one person is overpowered by sleep and the otherone not. Though the opponent agrees with this still the difficulty remains intact. Because, how does a person know that the disorganization of consciousness is due to the influence of sleep? Someone answers that by 'distinctness' and 'indistinctness' of the cognition difference can be maintained between the both states.[28] Vācaspati Miśra hold the same view that indirectly the object of a dream knowledge refers to an external object.[29] And these external objects are real.[30] He is of the view that it is some kind of *doṣa* either of the object or of the organ or of the mind which causes the knowledge in dream or illusion.[31]

Vṛttikāra Viśvanātha holds the same view like Gautama, Vātsyā yana and others.32. He further clarifies his stand by saying that though sometimes the perception like ' a person's head is being cut off by himself' which is absurd, occurs in dream which was never apprehended earlier, still it is due to wrong apprehension of relation as in the case of any other wrong knowledge of the awakened state. But in any case, such dream knowledges have real base in the external world.[33] Udayanācārya says in his *Nyāyakusumāñjali* that *svapna* (dream) is *smaraṇa* Because, the impressions of the objects, experienced earlier arouse this type of illusory knowledge.[34] The commentator Varadarāja also supports the same view. He says that though the functions of the sense-organs are absent still, the mind being prompted by the impressions of the experienced objects remember in dream.[35] Bhāsaravajña, the author of *Nyāyasāra* defines *viparyaya as mithyā-adhyavsāya* (i.e. the perverse-knowledge) and gives two examples namely, the perception of two moons at a glance and the perception of an elephant in sleep.[36]

Further, the commentator Vāsudeva clarifies in his commentary *Padapañcikā* why the author has given two examples? He says the intention of the author is to understand the difference of all perverse-knowledges and to refute the stand of the Vaiśeṣikas those who are of the opinion that dream-knowledge is something other than the *saṁśaya* (doubt), *viparyaya* (perverse), *Pramiti* (valid-knowledge) and *smaraṇa* (remembrance).[37]

According to this commentator *svapna* is *pramā* (valid-knowledge) since we feel pleasure which is produced by *bandhudarśana* (from the meeting of friend).[38]

Aparārkadeva, the other commentator of *Nyāyasāra* talks about the external reality of the dream-objects. In his Nyāyamuktāvali he points out that after getting up from sleep a person relates that "My son has been perceived by me closely in dream today though he resides in a far distance." By this statement those who think that the dream is a knowledge having no object have been defeated. Because, had there been no objects, that type of knowledge would not have arisen in the mind of a person. This knowledge cannot be classified under either *asatkhyāti* (unreal-knowledge) or *anā lambanakhyāti* (the knowledge without object).[39]

In the *Nyāyabūṣaṇa* the author Bhāsaravajña points out the criteria of reality of the object. According to him if an object possesses these three qualities namely, *arthakriyākāritva* (i.e. the constant behaviour), *saṁvāditva* (i.e one-to-one correspondence with the existent object) and *Upalabdhitva* (real apprehension) then that can be treated as real. Here too we find the contrast between the Idealists and the realists. Bhāsaravajña is of the opinion that any object of any knowledge will be true provided that stands scrutiny under above mentioned criteria. And if the object of knowledge is real it must cause a true-knowledge. It is also improper to establish the non-reality of one state by showing the instance of other state as corroboration which is utterly contrary.[40]

Keśava Miśra says that in dream all knowledges are false remembrance. Because of *doṣa* (fault) a wrong-knowledge arises i.e. in place of that type of natural-knowledge this type of wrong-knowledge is produced.[41]

Jayanta Bhaṭṭa regards the object of dream-knowledge as real. He also asserts that in the case of the example like 'a person perceives in dream that his head is being cut off' which is absolutely not possible to be experienced in real life, still, this vision may occur and that knowledge is real. Because, an object or a sight which has not been experienced can be cognised in dream.[42] What he wants to say that the object of a dream knowledge is not an unreal as sky-flower. Now, the Prabhākara Mīmāṁsakas raise question by saying that an object which has not been experienced by you how do you say that object is real?[43] In reply Jayanta says it may not be experienced by me but it will be experienced by somebody else. And hence, the object of that knowledge is real. On the otherhand, since the experience of a person cannot be remembered by other person so you (Prabhākara-Mīmāṁsakas) cannot establish dream as representative (i.e. remembrance)- says Jayanta Bhaṭṭa.[44] According to us (Naiyāyikas) dream is a direct perception and not remembrance. Because, *smṛti* (memory knowledge) remains ever obscure since it gets eroded[45]. In the *pratyakṣa-khaṇḍa* of the *Tattvacintāmaṇi* Gaṅgeśa admits *svapna* (i.e. the dream-knowledge) is mental creation and illusory by nature.[46] In the *Anumānakhaṇḍa* again he says that the *nidra* (sleep) is the *sahakārikāraṇa* (instrumental-cause) of the experience of the external-objects in dream.[47]

Analysis of dream in Vaiśeṣika system of philosophy:

A host of writers on *Vaiśeṣika-sūtras* of Kaṇāda namely, Praśastapāda, Jayanārāyaṇa, Śaṅkara etc. have stated about the epistemology of the dream-knowledge, which I have incorporated in that chapter which deals with the epistemology of the dream-knowledge.

The other writers' views regarding dream are as follows:

Nyāyakandalīkāra Śrīdhara regards dream as presentative in character. Because, dream-knowledges are independent from previously obtained experience. In other words, dream-knowledge is not mere reproduction of the past experience. And when all peripheral organs have retired to the central sensory organ at that time this knowledge is produced by mind. So this knowledge is originated by mind.[1] He further clarifies his stand by saying that the dream-knowledge, arising from the impressions of the objects experienced earlier is direct presentation *(aparokṣasaṁvedanākā ram)* of the objects which have no real existence at that time and place.[2] So, from this we may deduce that the knowledge of dream is unreal.

Praśastapāda categorises this knowledge as *avidyā* (illusion). And out of four *avidyās* as it is discussed in the *Praśastapādabhā sya* namely, *saṁśaya* (doubt), *viparyaya* (perverse), *anadhyavasā ya* (non-knowledge) and *svapna* (dream), this is one.[3]

He also says that three factors are involved in its production namely, *saṁskāra* (impression), *dhātudoṣa* (the defect or partly derangement of the humours) and *adṛṣṭa* (the unseen merit). And being caused by any one of these three factors what sort of vision one may have in dream also stated herein.[4]

Udayana holds the same view as it is held by Śrīdhara that though this knowledge is not produced by the external-organs still in dream we apprehend like direct perception e.g. I see the object determinately by means of my eyes etc. This type of awareness takes place in dream.[5] He also asserts that even if this knowledge is perceptual by nature which is perceived by the internal sense-organ i.e. the mind alone, still very rarely it assumes the form of inference with the help of probans *(Liṅga)*. For instance, in dream after seeing smoke in a particular place we can decide the existence of fire there.[6] Udayana has made a clearcut distinction between the dream (knowledge (which is perverse according to him) and the perversive knowledge of the awakened state. Because, in the awakened-state this *viparyaya* is produced by external-organs but in the dream-state that *viparyaya* is produced by mind alone. Again, in dream, knowledge is definite one because mind doesnot oscillate between alternative possibilities but in the waking state that happens very much.[7]

Śaṅkara Miśra, the author of *Vaiśeṣika-sūtra-Upaskāra* firmly states that the dream-knowledge is nothing but remembrance. And to support his view he has fingered out similarities of dream with remembrance (i.e. *smṛti*). He says that the epistemology of both the knowledges are one and the same. As remembrance is produced out of the particular type of contact between the soul, mind and impression so also the knowledge of dream is produced.[8] Again, the knowledge which arises in dream, in the form of remembrance the very same object is also experienced. So how to maintain the very nature of dream-knowledge as perceptual?[9]

In reply to these questions he has quoted the *Praśastapādabhā ṣya* and the *vṛtti* of Bharadvāja. Their reasonings are as follows:

(i) Praśastapāda says: 'The dream-knowledge is remembrance because it looks back to the past knowledge.'

(ii) Vṛttikāra says: 'since in dream only the experienced objects appear as flash so this knowledge cannot be designated anything other than *smṛti*'.[10]

NOTES & REFERENCES

1. *Svapnaviṣayābhimānavad ayam pramāṇaprameyābhimānaḥ (Nyā. Sū. 4.2.31)*
2. *Smṛtisaṁkalpavacca svapnaviṣayābhimānaḥ (Nyā. Sū. 4. 2.34)*
3. *Yathā smṛtiśca saṁkalpaśca pūrva upalabdha viṣayau na tasya pratyākhyānāya kalpete tathā svapne viṣayagrahaṇam pūrva upalabdhaviṣayam na tasya pratyākhyānāya kalpate iti. (NBh. On Sū 4.2.34)*
4. *Evam dṛṣṭaviṣayaśca svapnānto jāgaritāntena.*

   Yaḥsuptaḥsvapnam paśyati sa eva jāgrat-svapna darśanāni pratisandhatte idam adrākṣam iti. Tatra jāgratbuddhivṛttivaśā t svapnaviṣaya abhimāno mithyā iti vyavasāyaḥ

5. *Ubhaya aviśeṣe tu sādhana anarthakyam. Yasya svapnānta jāgaritāntayoḥ aviśeṣah tasya svapna-visayābhimanavad iti sādhanam anarthakam tad āśraya pratyākhyānāt.*

6. *Atasmin taditi ca vyavasāyaḥpradhānāśrayaḥ.*
Apuruṣe sthāṇau puruṣo iti vyavasāyaḥ sa pradhānā śrayaḥ
na khalu puruṣe' nupalabdhe puruṣa iti aparuṣe vyavasāyo bhavati, evam svapnaviṣayasya vyavasāyo.

7. *Tattvajñānena ca mithyā upalabdhir nivartyate, na arthaḥ.*

8. *Smṛtisaṁkalpavacca svapnaviṣayābhimānaḥ māyā gandharvanagara mṛgatṛṣṇikāvadvā iti na, pramāṇabhāvāt. (NV on Sūno 4.2.33-34).*

9. *Svapnāntavad avidyamāneṣu viṣayeṣu abhimāna ityatra na hetuḥ ucyate iti.*

10. *Svapnānte ca asanto viṣayāḥ iti ko hetur iti?*

11. *Khyātir iti cet?*

12. *Ayam jāgrat avasthā upalabdhānām viṣayāṇām citta-vyatirekiṇām asattve hetuḥ khyāti svapnavad iti*

13. *Na dṛṣṭāntasya sādhya asamatvāt.*

14. *Ya ete svapnāvasthāyām viṣayāḥ khyānti na te citta-vyatiriktā ityatra ko hetuḥ?*

15. *Pratibuddhena anupalambhād na santi iti.*

16. *Atha manyase yasmāt pratibuddhena na upalabhyante tasmād na santi iti.*

17. *Na, viśeṣaṇa upādānāt ye pratibuddhena upalabhyante te santi iti prāptam. Vyartham vā viśeṣaṇam pratibuddhena anupalambhād iti.*

18. *Yadi ca upalabhyamānam jāgrad avasthāyām svapnāvasthāyām viṣayam asantam manyase atha cittam asti iti atra ko hetur iti?*

19. *Viparyaye ca sāmarthyābhāvād hetuṛ jāgrato nupalabdher iti.*

20. *Yad upalabdhiḥsattva sādhanam tato 'nupalabdhiḥ asattvam sādhayati, viparyaye hi hetoḥ sāmarthyam dṛṣṭam iti*

21. *Na citta vyatirekiṇo............ tathāpi catvāroḥ skandhā iti.*

22. *Atha catuṣṭam na pratipadyate dṛṣṭam vijñānamātram eva abhyupagamyate. So 'pi dṛṣṭam vijñānabhedam anuyoktavyaḥ-vāhyasya adhyātmikasya ca vijñāna-bhedahetor abhāvāt katham vijñānabheda iti.*

23. *Svapnavad vijñānabhedam yadi pratipadyate, so 'pi dṛstānubhūtānām bhāvānām bhāvanāvaśena vijñānabhedam pratipādayitavyaḥ*

24. *Atha svapnapakṣe'pi bhāvanābhedād vijñanabhedam pratipadyet.*

So' pi bhāvya-bhāvaka vargayor bhedhena pratyavastheyaḥ na abhinnam bhāvyam bhāvakam ca iti.

25. *Ye ca ete svapnādipratyayāḥ pura-vimana-udyāna yānabhedhānuvidhāyinaḥ te mithyāpratyayā iti, mithyāpratyayānām ca jāgrat avasthā pratyaya-sāmānyād bhāvaḥ*

26. *Cittavyatiriktam viṣayam apratipadyamāno jāgratsvapnā vasthayor bhedam parynuyojyaḥ-jāgrat avasthāyām viṣayāḥ na santi svapnāvasthāyām apiti iyam svapnāvasthā iyam jā grat avasthā iti kuto etat?*

27. *Dharma adharma vyavasthā ca na prāpnoti; yathā svapnāvasthāyām gamyāgamanāt dharmotpattir na bhavati evam jāgrat avasthāyām api na syāt.*

28. *Atha nidrā upaghātānupaghātau bhedam janayata iti pratipadyeta. Tadapi tādṛg eva, nidrā upaghātaḥ cetaso vaikṛtyahetur iti katham avagamyate? Atha vijñānasya spaṣṭatām aspaṣṭatām ca bhedam pratipadyeta.*

29. *Svapnajñānam api pārmparyeṇa bāhyanibandhanam itartha. (NVT on Sū No. 4.2.33-34)*

30. *Bāhyanimittatvam eva tu pāramārthikam ityāha.*

31. *Svapna-māyāgandhanagara-mṛgatṛṣṇādivijñāneṣu anuvartamānesu viṣayendriya manadoṣanimittatvam astu.*

32. *Pūrva upalabdhaviṣaya.....smṛtyādi....(Vṛ on Sū 4.2. 32-33)*

33. *Na ca svapne...... nijaśiraḥkhaṇḍanam paśyati,*
Na tu idam pūrva upalabdham iti......
Saṁsargabhānaṣya ca bhrāntatvāt.
Bhramasyapi sadvisayatva asti.

34. *(Svapnāvasthāyām katham jñānam iti cet) tat tat saṁskāra udbodhe viṣayasmaraṇena svapnavibhramānām utpatteḥ (Nyā kū pp. 323-24)*

35. *Indriyavyāpārābhāve' pi pūrvānubhavajanita-*
saṁskāra udbodha prabhāvita tat tat viṣaya-
smaraṇa sahakṛtam manaḥsvapnabhramān
utpādayati iti (Ibid, pp. 324)

36. *Mithyā 'dhyavasāyo viparyayaḥ tad yathā, dvau candrau iti, suptasya gajādidarśanam ca iti. (Nyā sā p. 5)*

37. *Sakalaviparyaya-prabheda avabodhārtham udāharaṇa dvayam uktam. Vaiśeṣikāḥ khalu saṁśaya-viparyaya-pramiti smaraṇebhyo vilakṣanam svapnajñānam manyate. (Nyā Pañ* p. 5)

38. *Svapne bandhudarśanajanitasukhānubhavastu pramā. (Ibid. p. 5)*

39. *Yathā pratibuddhaḥ san kathayati 'Mayā adya svapne deśā ntaratyo'pi putraḥ sannihito dṛṣṭaḥ' evam ca anā lambanam eva svapnajñānam iti ye manyante,*
to parākṛtāḥ. Na ca evam asatkhyāti; anālambana-
khyātir vā prasajyate. (Nyā. Muktā. p. 62)

40. *Nyāyabhūṣaṇa, ed. Varanasi, 1968, p. 150.*

41. *Svapne ca sarvam eva jñānam smaranam ayathārtham.*

Doṣavaśena tat iti sthāne idam iti udayāt. (Tar. bhā. p. 190)

42. *Asad na pratibhāti iti ucyate, na tu ananu bhūtam iti. (Nyā. Mañ p. 469)*

43. *Ananubhūtam sat katham jānīṣe?*

44. *Mayā tad na anubhūtam, anyenānubhaviṣyate. Parānubhūte tu smaraṇam aghatamānaṁ iti (Ibid p. 470)*

45. *Anubhava pratyayaśca svapnam saṁvedyate, na smaraṇānullekhamātram iti..... smṛtipramoṣa samarthanam. iti. (Ibid).*

46. *Svapnavibhramavat svotprekṣitapadārtha...... mānaso 'yam. (T.C. p. 804)*

47. *Nidrāsahakāreṇa bāhyasvapnānubhava (Ibid, p. 35)*

1. *Pūrvādhigama anapekṣam paricchedasvabhāvam mānasam manomātraprabhavam tat svapnajñānam. (Nyā Kan. p. 437)*
2. *Saṁskārācca pūrvānubhūtaviṣayād asatsu deśa kālavyavahiteṣu viṣayeṣu pratyakṣākāram aparoksasaṁvedanākāram svapnajñānam (Ibid. p. 439)*
3. *Tatra avidyā caturvidhā saṁe anadhyavasāya-svapna lakṣaṇā. (Praśasta. bhā. p. 411)*
4. *Saṁskārapātavāddhātudoṣād adṛṣṭācca... Ibid p. 430)*
5. *Yatra asatyāpi cakṣurādivyāpāre caksuṣā .... imam artham paśyāmi........iti anuvyavasāyah svapnajñānam. (Kir. p. 180)*
6. *Indriyadvāreṇaiva pratyakṣākāṛam sākṣātkarotīti ca upalakṣaṇam. Liṅgadvāreṇa eva anumityākāram kvacid ityapi draṣṭavyam; Yathasmin deśe dhūmād agnir iti.... (Ibid p. 181)*
7. Ayathārthatve' pyuratendriyagrāmasvabhāvād-viparyayād vyavacchedaḥ(Ibid. p. 180)
8. *Yathā ātmamanasoḥ saṁyogaviśeṣāt saṁskārāt ca smṛtiḥtathā svapnajñānam api ityarthaḥ. (Upa. on Vai. Sū No. 9. 2.7)*

9. *Nanu yajjñānam svapnamadhye svapnajñānānubhūtasya eva arthasya smṛtirupam jāyate tatra svapnatvam na vartate svapnasya anubhavarūpatvāt... (Ibid.)*

10. *(a) Taduktam Praśastadevācāryaiḥ-'atitajñānapratyavekṣaṇāt smṛtireva 'iti'*
(b) Uktam ca vṛttikāraiḥ-anubhūtavastuṣphuraṇārtha-tayā na smaraṇād arthāntaram svapnajñānam iti. (Ibid. No. 9.2.8)

III.4 POSITION IN BUDDHISM:

The theory of knowledge in Buddhism with reference to Dream-knowledge:

At the very early-stage Buddhism branched-out into eighteen schools but got settled into only four principal schools namely, Vaibhāṣika, Sautrāntika, Yogācāra and Mādhyamika. Whether these four schools came into existence side by side or one after another is still a question of debate says Prof. Chatterji.[1]

Out of these four Philosophical schools of Buddhism, Vaibhā ṣika and Sautrāntika belong to the Hinayāna-fold and remaining two belong to the Mahāyāna-fold.[2]

According to the Vaibhāṣika school external objects are directly perceived. They admit the reality of the external entities though they acknowledge them momentarily. They hold the view that "our knowledge or awareness of things is not creation but only discovery"[3] They further argue that if it is not the case of perception then the invariable concomitance *(vyāpti)* between the Probans and Probandum would be impossible on which the inferencial knowledge is based.[4]

On the contrary, the Sautrāntika school is of the opinion that we infer the existence of the external object and what we directly perceive is nothing but our idea which assumes the form of the external object *(sākārajñāna)*. In other words, the contact of the sense-organ with an object produces a knowledge to which the object of knowledge transfers its form and it is only because of the form of that object the existence of that can be inferred.[5] This doctrine is otherwise known as '*nityānumeyabāhyārthavāda*'[6]. This has also been designated as '*sākārajñānavāda*'[7]. This school also admit the momentarily existence of outwardly entities. According to the follower of this school of thought a cognition *(jñāna)* is both revealer (i.e. *grāhaka)* and revealed (grāhya).[8]

So we may say that the Sautrāntika school is the strong believer of the 'representative' theory of knowledge, and this can be compared with the theory of Locke in western tradition. On the other hand, the Vaibhāṣika school is the follower of the 'Presentative' theory of the knowledge.[9] Of course, Prof. Stcherbatsky does not agree with this view. He says: "There is no great disagreement between the Vaibhāṣikas *(sarvāstivādins)* and the Sautrāntikas on the interpretation of the origin of cognition."[10]

It is widely accepted that both schools were closely associated. The propounder of the Sautrāntika school was Kumāralat. But his treatise in original is not available to us. In Sautrāntika group we get as many as four writers namely, Kumāralat, Srīlat, Buddhadeva and Dharmatrāt. Though we get the references of their works like *Kalpanamanditikā, Vibhāṣāśāstra* etc. in the history of Buddhist literature, still it is a matter of pity that we do not have anyone of their original work.[11] In the *Abhidharmakośabhāṣya* of Vasubandu we find some quotations referring to the views of Sautrā ntikas.[12]

The doctrine of the Yogācāras is *Vijñānavāda*. They do not accept the reality of the external world. According to them the external objective world is the transformation of internal consciousness *(Vijñānavipariṇāma)*. They divide cognition into two heads.[13]

(i) *Ālayavijñāna:* This is a chain of continuous consciousness. This is identified with the notion of 'self' (i.e. *ahamāspadam)* This type of *vijñāna* is neither steady nor permanent by nature. It gets generated owing to the chain of continuity *(santāna)* of the basic consciousness in every moment and each product differs from the other one. *Ālayavijñāna* is the *Pramāta* (knower) and only real according to them.

(ii) *Pravṛttivijñāna:* This is the knowledge of the external world viz. the knowledge of red, blue etc. In short, all *prameyas* (objects) which undergo changes all the while belong to this category.[14] Advayavajra again in *'Tattvaratnāvali' of Advayavajrasaṁgraha* has made two distinct divisions of the Yogācāra school. One school is the follower of *sākāravāda* and the other school follows *nirākā ravāda* (i.e. the cognition has no shape at all).[15]

In the first case the cognition itself serves the purposes of the external entities. One need not posit external entities. But in the second case, due to the absence of the form of cognition no external entity can be postulated since there is no other means of cognising entity other than cognition. So cognition must have form and that is to be accepted.[16] Nirākāravādins hold the view that there is no such external reality of the object, which is accepted by the ignorant people. It is only consciousness, which is internal being influenced by *Vāsanā* (impression) appears as external object. And these are nothing but *māyā* (illusion). Cognition is formless but it has self-illuminating character. Cognition is free from any sort of imprint or stain of the postulated external objects and as clear as sky and infinite.[17]

The Bauddhadarsana in the *Sarvadarśanasaṁgraha* further views that from the metaphysical point of view yogācāra school is the follower of the advaitins. Tentatively they have posited some notions like agent, object etc. without which day-to-day cannot be explained.[18]

Mādhyamikas go a step further from the Yogācāras. They discard the *vijñāna* also. According to them a cognitioin is devoid of object. They are the followers of *sūnyavāda* (nihilism). The opinion, which they hold is, reality neither existent nor non-existent nor the combination of both nor the negation of both:

They classify reality into two groups:

(a) *Paramārthasatya and (b) samvṛtisatya.*

To them the first one is the ultimate reality. And the second one is relative one which refers to our everyday experience and it is characterised by our notion of name, namable, cognition, cognisable etc.[19]

Further, *saṁvṛtisatya* is divided into two heads. (i) *Tathyasaṁvṛti and (ii) mithyāsaṁvṛti.* when a knowledge of blue is produced as blue out of the contact of sense-organ that is called *tathyasaṁvṛti.* And due to some deffect either in object or sense-organ, under that circumstances when a knowledge is produced that is called *mithyāsaṁvṛti.* In short, any sort of halucinatory-knowledge they classify under this category.[20]

The Vaibhāṣikas and the Sautrāntikas are realists to a great extent but the Yogācāras and the Mādhyamikas are idealists. Of course, from the trancendental point of view everything is unreal according to them. And this notion is shared equally by some of the Buddhists and the Vaidāntins.

This is in brief, their views regarding the knowledge of the external-world. Now, we shall deal with dream-knowledge according to them.

Yogācāras on dream-knowledge:

We do not find any notable opinion of Diṅnāga in his available treatises viz. *Pramāṇasamuccaya (Pratyakṣākhaṇḍa), Nyāyapraveśa, Ālambanaparīkṣā etc.* But he defines *pratyakṣa* as 'kalpanāpoḍham' (i.e. the perception which is other than vikalpa). Dharmakīrti defines *pratyakṣa* as 'Kalpanāpoḍham abhrāntam'. So since Diṅnāga did not include *abhrānta* in the defination of perception, it may be held that illusory-knowledge like dream was not a perceptual knowledge. *Nyāyapañcika*, a commentary on *Nyā yapraveśavṛtti* speaks about the objectless nature of dream-knowledge.[21] Dharmakīrti did not say anything about *svapna* in his *Nyāyabindu*. But the commentators like Dharmottarācārya and Durvekmiśra held this knowledge as *apramā* (non-valid-knowledge).[22] *Pramāṇavārtika* of Dharmakīrti also observes that dream-knowledge is objectless. In other words, the knowledge of this phenomenon is not real. Because, this knowledge is not associated with real object. And when the object of knowledge is non-existent it certainly produces unreal-knowledge.[23] He further says that though the dream-knowledge is remembrance still it cannot be on par with the remembrance of the awakening state. Manoratha Nandin clarifies it in his *Vṛtti* by saying that we remember the object of dream knowledge faintly like the object of an indeterminate perception *(Nirvikalpakānubhūti)*.[24] Dharmapāla, a commentator of the *Ālambana-Parīkṣa* of Diṅnāga tries to establish their school's view showing dream-knowledge as an example. He says: consciousness has no support in the external world, as it is revealed in dream-knowledge (i.e. dream-knowledge has no object, existent externally.)[25]

Yogācāras do not differ the object of dream-state from the object of the awakened-state. Both states are treated equally by them. [26]

Madhyamikas on dream-knowledge:

Nāgārjuna says in his *Madhyamakaśāstra* that the dream-knowledge is an illusion.[27] Because, this is a knowledge without corresponding the object, existent externally. *Prasannapadā*, a commentary on *Madhyamakakārikās* by Chandrakīrtti, reiterates the same view. Śāntarakṣit, the well-known writer of this school says *svapna* is a mental-knowledge. This knowledge does not require the help of *cakṣus* (eyes) in its generation. This is caused by earlier-knowledge *(Pūrvabuddhi)*. In short, the knowledge of the awakened-state acts as material cause *(upādāna-kāraṇa)* in its formation.[28]

Again, he describes about the nature of this knowledge. He says dream-knowledge appears as constantly behavable *(arthakriya-bhāsi).* But it cannot be treated as valid- knowledge *(Pramāṇa)* At the same time we cannot categorize this knowledge as illusion. Because, this is a knowledge which is caused by the outwardly existent entity.[29] Vaibhāṣikas hold dream-knowledge as *avijña*pti (ajñā na).[30] About Sautrāntika we do not have any data by which any assertion can be made regarding their stand on dream-knowledge.

NOTES AND REFERENCES

1. Chatterji, D.C. "The Problem of knowledge and the four school of later Buddhism", *ABORI* Poona, 1931, Vol. XII, Part 3, pp. 207.
2. Shastri, D.N. "The Sautrāntika Theory of Knowledge", *ABORI*, Poona, Vol. XXXII, 1952.
3. Radhakrishnan, S., *Indian Philosophy*, Vol. I. 2nd edition, 1929, pp. 614.
4. *Prātyakṣikasya Kasyacid api arthasyābhāvena-vyāptisaṁvedanasthānābhāvena anumāna Pravṛtti anupapattiḥ.......* (Sarva, D. Saṁ. pp. 43)
5. *Indriyasannikṛṣṭasya visayasyotpādye jñāne* svākāra samarpakatayā samarpitena cākāreṇa tasyārthasya anumeyatopapatteh, (Sarva,. D. Saṁ pp. 36)
6. *Nyā, Mañ. pp. 41*
7. Ibid., pp. 41
8. Ibid.,
9. "The Sautrāntika Theory of Knowledge", op. cit. pp. 123.
10. Stcherbatsky, Th., *Central conception of Buddhism, p. 63*
11. Upādhyāya, Baladeva, *Bhāratīya Darśna*, pp. 192-215.
12. Cf. *Abhidharmakośabhāṣya* (Pradhan's edition)
13. Sharma, R.R., "The Yogācāra Theory of the External World", Vol. II., pp. 893.

14. ....*kṣane kṣane praliyamānam utpadyamānam cālayavijñā nam............... viliyamānā utpadyamānā ca svabhāvena suranaranārakarūpena......prameyam etc. (Sarva. M. Saṁ pp. 19)*

15. *Tattvaratnāvali of Advayavajrasaṁgraha, pp. 18.*

16. *Dhiyo nīlādirūpatve bāhyo' rthaḥkimnibandhanaḥ Dhiyo' nī lādirūpatve bāhyo' rthaḥ...(This is the view of Dharmakīrti) Ibid, pp. 18.*

17. *Bāhyo na vidyate hyartho yathā bālai vāsanāluṭhitam cittam arthābhāsam.....yāvad ābhāsate yacca tān māyā iva bhāsate.... (Adv. Saṁ. p. 18)*

18. ....Vastuto vedyavedakākāravidhurāyā api buddher vyavahartṛparijñānānurodhena vibhinnagrāhyagrāhakākāra rupavattayā. (Sarva. D, Saṁ. pp. 32-33).

19. Ajñānam hi samantāt sarvapadārtha tattvāvacchādanāt saṁvṛti ityucyate, sa ca abhidhāna-abhidheya jñāna jñeyādi lakṣanā....
(Prasannapadā on Mad. Kā pp. 215)
.................Paramārtham. (Mad. kā 24.10)

20. Sa ca samvṛtirdvividhā lokata eva, tathyasaṁvṛtir mithyāsaṁvṛtiśceti. Tathā hi kiṁcit pratityajātam nīlādikam vasturupam.....satyam.... doṣavadindriyopalabdham................ eva mithyā.
(Bodhi, pañjikā. 9th chap, Sū No. 2)

21. Jñānam saṁvedanam, tacca nirviṣayam........(Nyā. Pra. Vṛ. 35)
Nirviṣayam apīti svapnādau nirgocaram api ityartha.
(Pancikā on Nyā Pra. Vṛ. p. 76)

22. Yathā ardharātre madhyāhnakāla vastugrāhi svapnajñānam na ardharātrakāle vastuni pramāṇam
(Pradīpaḥpp. 25)

23. Sarvajñāna arthavattvāccet svapnādau anyathā[illegible]ṣaṇāt
..............(Pra. vā Prat. Khan. pp. 106)

24. Svapne'pi smaryate smārtam na ca tat tādṛg[illegible]arthavat.
(Ibid . pp 184)
Na ca tat prabodhāvasthāyām tādṛgarthavad yādṛso

nirvikalpenānubhūto' arthastādṛsārthena yuktam smaryate. (Vṛtti, pp. 184)

25. Vijñānasya na bāhyavastu ālambanam- yathā svapnāvasthāyām prakāśamānam. (Ālam. Parī. pp. 38)

26. Dṛstārthavyavahāraśca svapnavyavahāravat saṁvṛtyā saṁgacchate. (Sarva. D. Saṁ pp. 29)

27. Yathāmāyā yathā svapno gandharvanagaram yathā (Mad. Kā 7.34)
Yathā māyādayaḥ* svabhābena anupapannā..... (Prasannapadā, pp. 75)

28. Svatantrā mānasī buddhiḥcaksurādi anapekṣaṇāt. Svopādānabalenaiva svapnādāviva vartate. (Tat. Saṁ. Sloko. No. 1929)

29. Nanu ca arthakriyābhāsi jñānam svapne' pi vidyate. Na ca tasya pramāṇatvam tad hetoḥ prathamasya ca. Na evam bhrā ntā hi sā' vasthā bāhyānibandhanā. (Ibid. Sloka, No. 2978-2980)

30. Abhīkṣṇaṁ tadālambanacetanābhyāsāt svapneṣu api tā (avijñapti) anusaṅginyo bhavanti. (Abhi. Ko. bhā p. 197).

III. 5. POSITION IN JAINISM

Jainas hold that svapna is of two types:

(i) *Svastha* (i.e. caused by goodhealth) and

(ii) *Asvastha* (i.e. caused by ill-health). They have defined them as follows:

(i) *Svasthasvapna:* When all *dhātus* namely, *vāta, pitta and kapha* are in their equilibrium state, *svasthasvapna* occurs.

(ii) *Asvasthasvapna:* On the contrary, when these *dhātus* are in unbalanced state i.e. anyone of these is either increased or decreased, *asvasthasvapna* takes place.[1] Thus, it implies that dream, in Jaina literature, is analysed in terms of *dhātus*. And this is in conformity with the analysis in the *Āyurveda*. Now, question arises:

how do we know that dream occurs? This is answered by saying that knowledge occurs in the soul and the soul knows it.[2]

As regard the validity of dream-knowledge, the Jainas hold that a dream knowledge is false when it is a product of *dhātudoṣa*. On the otherhand, a dream-knowledge is true if it is produced by *daiva*.[3]

Dream has correspondence with reality. Because, objects, which are perceived and felt in our day-to-day life can alone appear in dream. In other words, it is not objectless *(nirā lambanajñāna)*.[4] Apart from those two causes which are pointed out earlier namely, *daiva* and bodily order or disorder, Jaina thinkers point out some more causes which bring about dreams intio existence.

They have classified them into seven categories:[5]

(i) Based upon previous experience *(Anubhūtam)*

(ii) Observation in the awakening state *(Dṛṣṭaḥ)*

(iii) Constant thinking *(Vicintitaḥ)*

(iv) Hearing *(Śrutaḥ)*

(v) Meritorious activities *(Puṇyam)*

(vi) Sinful act *(Pāpam)* and (vii) Place *(Pradeśaḥ)*

If we observe critically we find that the causes of dreams enumerated in the earlier paragraph somewhat overlap and they are not distinct.

The impact of these nine types of dreams caused by nine causes can be either auspicious or inauspicious and either fruitful or fruitless.[6]

Like the Āyurvedins Jainas also hold that a person in sleeping-cum-waking state experiences dream. In other words, this is the state of a dreamer where he remains half-sleep and half-awakened.[7] In Jaina traditional literature we get the references about symbolic dreams. *Kalpasūtra*[8] enumerates fourteen dream objects as auspicious* and these are termed as symbols since they used to forecast omens in a symbolic way. They are as follows:

"Gaya vasaha siha abhiseya
Dāma sasi dinayaram jyayam kumbham.
Paumasara sāgara vimāṇa
Bhavaṇa rayaṇuccaya sihim ca".

Fourteen auspicious objects are "an elephant, an ox, a lion, anointment, a garland, the moon, the sun, an ensign, a jar, a lotus lake, a sea, celestial abode *(vimāṇa-bhavaṇa)* a heap of gems and a burning flame." Those dream symbols were interpreted by the experts. In their terminology they have been designated as *sūviño* lakkhaṇa padhaga.[9] (i.e. the interpreter of the objective dream symbols).

In Jaina system of Philosophy we find that the Jaina thinkers were aware of the sub-conscious state of mind, which is the source of dream. In the *mallakadṛṣṭānta* (an example of an earthen pot) they have pointed out the sub-conscious state of mind by saying that if a person pours water in a pot continuously, that starts absorbing till the limit of saturation is arrived, then the water becomes visible. According to them the absorbent part of the pot can be compared with the subconscious-state of mind. As water remains in an invisible form in the absorbent part of the pot, so also our suppressed desires, which are dissatisfied remain dormant in the sub-conscious-state of mind and rear up to the conscious-state in the form of a dream.[10] Taking into consideration all aspects of dream phenomenon *Bhagawatisūtra* has classified dream under the following five heads.[11]

(i) *Yathātathyasvapna:* Dream-vision which has one to one correspondence with external reality. The criterion of its reality is that the contents or the constituent parts of the dream must convey 1:1 relationship with the external object which has appeared in dream.

(ii) *Pratānasvapna:* Dream-knowledge caused by the remification (i.e. by branching out some similar facts of dreams) of dream-visions.

(iii) *Cintāsvapna:* Dream-visions occur in accordance with the thought of the awakening-state. e.g. If a person hears the warfare between Karṇārjuna thinks too much about their vigour which may appear in dream during sleep.

(iv) *Tadviparita:* A dream-knowledge, which is utterly opposite to reality.

(v) *Avyaktadarśana:* Some sort of dream-vision which cannot be expressed through language.

NOTES AND REFERENCES

1. *Te ca svapnā dvidhāmnātaḥ svasthāsvasthā... samaistu dhā tubhiḥsvasthā viṣamaiḥitare matāḥ(Ādipurāṇa 41/59)*
2. *.....svasthāsvasthātmagocarāḥ (Ādipurāṇa 59)*
3. *.........Dosaprakopajāmithyā tathyāḥsyurdaivasaṁbhavā (Ādipurāṇa. 61)*
4. *Svapnajñānam* api anubūta dṛṣṭādi arthaviṣayatvād, na nirā lambanam. (Syādvādamañjarī. 16/235)
5. *Viśeṣāvāśyakabhāṣyam with Śiṣyahita Bṛhadvṛtti, Benaras ed. 1914.*
6. *Kalghatgi, T.G., "Dreams In Jain Psychology" pp. 38*
7. *Sikder, J.C. Studies in The Bhagawatisūtra, pp. 582*
8. *Kalpasūtra of Bhadrabahu Svāmi pp. 6*

* According to śvetāmbara tradition those fourteen objects are auspicious. On the otherhand, Digāmbara tradition accepts sixteen objects as auspicious by aidding two more objects namely, *siṁhāsana and Nāgabhavaṇa.*

9. *"Dreams In Jaina Psychology", op. cit. pp. 38.*

10. *Nandisuttam of Devavācaka,*

11. *Studies In The Bhagawatisūtra, op. cit. pp. 582.*

CHAPTER-IV

ANATOMY AND PHYSIOLOGY OF DREAM

IV.0 *ANATOMY AND PHYSIOLOGY OF DREAM*

Suśruta holds the view that living beings are overpowered by sleep. Our common notion is this that each and every being is in possession of three qualities. *Sattva, Rajas, and Tamas.* Of course, degree of possession varies in each individual. When the human heart, which is the locus of consciousness, is captivated by *tamas*, at that time he gets sleep.

Vāgbhaṭṭa says "When all the *srotas* (channels) belonging to the organism are filled with phlegm *(kapha)* and the sense-organs, being tired, retire from the field of action, then sleep overpowers a man."

Sleep is a *vṛtti* of *manas* where there is no existence of external object. Mind acquires this state due to the preponderance of *tamas*. According to the Indian Medical science, sleep is of three types.

(i) *Tāmasī Nidrā*

(ii) Svābhābikī Nidrā

(iii) Vaikārikī Nidrā.

(i) *Tāmasi Nidrā:* While carrying the impressions of cognitions, the nervous system is filled with phlegm and because of the intensity of *tamas*, sleep overpowers a living being. This sleep is designated as *Tāmasī Nidrā.* None wakes up from this sleep, being overpowered. Because this type of sleep takes place only at the time of final destruction *(Pralaya)*. This sleep is *Tāmasī* because in this state of sleep the preponderance of *Tamas* is more.

(ii) *Svābhābikī Nidrā:* This is the natural sleep of living beings.

When a person is in possession of *Sattva* quality then he gets this sleep. Being overpowered by *Rajas* one may have irregular sleep. Because the very nature of *Rajas* is *cala.*[1] But this natural sleep prevails in the midnight.

(iii) *Vaikārikī Nidrā:* One who possesses little phlegm and more wind he gets this type of sleep. In other words, when a person is exhausted after much exertion, mind retires to a place where there is no external objects. Meanwhile, the proportion of wind increases and phlegm decreases, at that time due to the intensity of wind he gets overpowered by this type of sleep. This sleep is called *Vaikārikī* . In order to corroborate this fact Dalhana has quoted one verse from *Carakasaṁhitā. "Yadā tu manasi klānte karmātmānaḥ klamā nvitāḥ. Viṣayebhya nibartante tadā svapiti mānavaḥ".* This sleep is again subdivided into two categories-*Svapna and Suṣupti.* Here *svapna* means dream-consciousness and *suṣupti* means dreamless sleep.[2] *Svapna* (Dream) is a specific state. The origin of *Svapna is Jā garitasthāna.* In Svapna *Jāgaritasthāna acts as saṁskāra.* It has no independent origin. So it is not primary but secondary phenomenon. *Svapna* is an experience accompanied by *viṣaya.* It occurs when all sense-organs are withdrawn from their usual function. This is the view of the *vedāntin.* The following conditions are required for the genesis of *svapna.*

(i) It is related to sense-organs.

(ii) It has origin in *jāgrata*-state.

The link between the two *(jāgrata and svapna)* is bridged by the continuity of experience. If we put these all required factors in a diagram then it will look like the following:

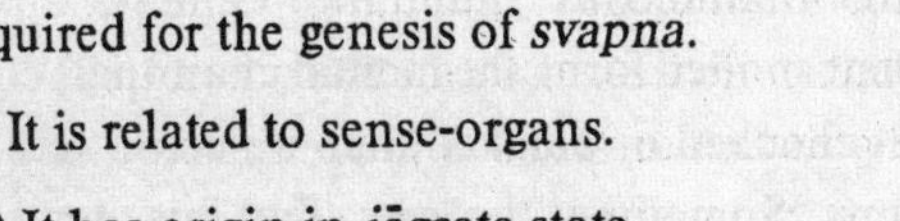

Here *saṁskāra* is the co-relating link between the two. In other words, *saṁskāra* produces *smṛti* and this *smṛti* is the inspiring factor in the formation of dream.

In the state of sleep half asleep person acquires opposite knowledge *(viparīta jñāna)*. The difference between *svapna* and *nidrā* is like this. *Nidrā=Svapna+ Suṣupti*, the quantity of this state is 1/2 *svapna + 1/2 suṣupti.*

Svapna—Nidrā—Suṣupti
↓
Co-relating factor

Svapna= *Nidrā + Svapna*, the quantity of this state

is 1/2 *nidrā + 1/2 svapna. Svapna is Ardhaprasupti-state, whereas Sleep is Pūrṇaprasupti-state.*

Because of *ardhaprasupti* two opposite aspects of knowledges are involved in it.

Jāgarita–Ardhaprasupti-Prasupti

Ardhaprasupti causes neither full sleep nor awakening. *Svapna* is primarily mental phenomenon of a specific type. This specification is caused by the dominent sense faculty. Because of this a person dreams various types of dream, both auspicious and inauspicious *(Ca. Saṁ 5.42).*

When all these three *dhātudoṣas* (humours) namely, *kapha, pitta and vāta* are in their spoiled form, the mental channnels completely or partially get chocked or blocked then a person sees all sorts of deadly dreams. Sometimes he sees that his death is approaching to him *(Ca. Saṁ. 5.41)*

One physiological aspect of *svapna* is this that it requires *rajoguṇa*. Due to the preponderance of *rajas, svapna* occurs. Sometimes dreams are related to past birth. From the store of past incidents mind may choose anyone it likes, sometimes good and sometimes bad. *(Su. Śari 4.36).* When all sense-organs are not fully active, it implies that they have lost their power, and are overpowered by *tamas*, though the person *(bhūtātmā)* is not sleeping but seems to be sleeping, *(Su. Śari. 4.37)*, at that time a dream takes place.

Svapna is related to *Anuparata* state of mind. *Uparatamanastvam* (Cessation of the function of mind outwardly) is sleep. *Anuparatamanastvam* is dream. To be more clear, at stage of dream the mind is active but internally, and not externally. And this is the vital time for the occurence of dream.[3]

1. Vide, *Sāṁkhyakārika*, No. 13
2. Mishra, Umesh, *"Dream Theory In Indian Thought."* p. 271-73
3. *Āyurvedīya Mahākoṣa*, p. 1685

IV.I Dream in Indian Medical Sciences

Dreams are of seven types-*Dṛṣṭaḥ* (Perceived), *Śrutaḥ* (Perceived through audiable organ), *Anubhūtaḥ*(Felt through perceptible organ), *Prārthitaḥ*(Desired), *Kalpitaḥ*(Conceived), *Bhāvikaḥ* (Wished), *Doṣajaḥ(Kapha, Pitta, Vāta* all three *dhātudoṣas* are its origin) *(Ca. Saṁ. 5.43)*.

Āyurveda has defined all these seven types of *svapna*. (i) *Dṛṣṭaḥ- In dṛīṣti* anatomical factor is eye, physiological factor is vision. It requires normal functioning faculty. It implies the functional link between the reality in dream and the actual experience. Whatever a person experiences in day-to-day life the same experience appears in his dream during sleep. In other words, the origin itself of this type of dream is based upon in our real life, in the awakened state. Dream will be related to consciousness, befitting to *rupa*.

(ii) *Śrutaḥ-* It requires anatomical factor ear. Audition is the normal functioning faculty, past participle mark relates to dream experience and factual experience.

(iii) *Anubhūtaḥ-* Whatever we realise in the awakening state the same is realized by the internal process of knowledge. In short, the mere reproduction of past experience.

(iv) *Prārthita-* It involves mental phenomena more. This is much related with wish, desire etc. This phenomenon is not so much anatomical but physiological, more psychological, mentally desired. Thirst etc. are mentally desired but not *kāma, krodha* etc. This phenomenon is beyond *dṛṣṭa and śutra.* This is related to inner consciousness.

(v) *Kalpita*-More than imaginary. Image means a kind of mental creation, which might have base in day-to-day reality. Not directly perceiveable but something imaginary. This type of phenomenon can never be apprehended either by six *pramāṇas, namely Pratyakṣa, Anumāna, Upamāna, Śabda, Anupalbdhi, and Arthāpatti.*

(vi) Bhāvika-'Want to become something' is its root cause. Being motivated by *bhābanā* person desires something.

(vii) *Doṣaja*-Three *dhātudoṣas* cause dream. *Vāta, Pitta, Kapha*-only three are indicated here. Apart from these physiological condition, temperament, bodily affairs may also cause dream. These are also related to *doṣaja-prakriti.* In relation with these three types of *dhātudoṣas,* a dream occurs. Reddish, Whitish, Bluish, Yellowish all these colours indicate humours like *Pitta, Kapha, Vāta and Vāta-Pitta* (combination of these two) respectively *(Arū. Ahṛśā 6.61).*

Qualitative and quantitative evaluation of dream:

Out of seven types of dream first five are fruitless. But a dream of this category occuring in the first part of night will become fruitful, partially. If a person is awakened after dream and does not sleep again he will have *mahāphala,* immediately, without much delay. After dreaming a bad dream if a person sees again a good dream, as a whole the effect will be good. So the sequence is a bad dream immediately followed by a good one brings a good result. If the object of a day time experience is seen in the dream at night and if it is prolonged or very short in duraton of time then it will be fruitless.

The dream belonging to the category of *Bhāvika* and *Doṣaja* will be fruitful and true.

Indication of death in dream:

In the dream he who rides on a donkey or an ass and goes towards southern direction, he will be caught by deadly disease and will die. He who sees an evil spirit in his dream, drinks wine along with a person, who is otherwise dead and who is drawn by a dog then he is immediately caught by fever and passes away. He who sees in dream sky of reddish colour tinged by lac, he is caught by disease like *'Raktapitta'* and dies. He who finds in dream that a thorny creeper is sprouting from some region of his heart, he is caught by a disease, called *'gulma'*.

In the dream being nacked when a person smeared with ghee, offers oblation in the fire and from whose chest the lotuses are sprouted, he is cought by skin disorder (leprosy). In dream, he who drinks a lot of oily substances with *candālas*, dies out of diabetes. He who dances with *Rakṣasas* in dream, will be dancing in rain in reality and being mad will pass away. In dream he who dances, being mad and takes away deadbody along with him will be caught by *Apasmā* (mental disorder). He who eats *Apūpa* (cake) dies by vomiting *(Ca. Ind. 5.8.40)*. He who walks in his dream along with donkey, camel, cat, monkey, tiger, pig, fox etc. dies.

Some other bad dreams are as follows:

If a person sees the eclipse of sun and moon in his dream, it causes *Akṣiroga*. If a person beholds falling down from the sun and moon in dream, he loses his eye-sight.

For a patient the following dream sights are inauspicious:

Sprouting out the creeper from his head, erection of the nest on his head by birds, his head is being cut off by himself, hovering of crows and vultures over his head, if any portion of his body is cut off either by these entities-cane, creeper, bambu, grass, thorn, falling of dust particles and ashes, especially of burnt bodies, dragging of himself into muddy water, streams are getting separated from each other, equipments of songs and dances, wearing red-coloured cloth he finds himself growing in age, limbs are growing by taking oil bath. in marriage he shaves himself, he takes rich cooked foods, oil, ghee and wine, vomiting, perspiring etc. If he obtains gold and iron in dream, these indicate misfortune. He will be cought and defeated. Slipers are being stolen, falling down, very joyful, laughing like anything-all these indicate something bad. He is being censured by provoked parents. If he sees in dream that planet, stars, tooth, eyes of the deities are falling down then destruction will come to him. Mountain is getting cracked and falling down, a forest started with red flower or the forest possesses red flower, appearing in dream means the dreamer entering into the realm of the sinful things. Likewise so many sights perceived in dream cause the total destruction of the dreamer. *(Ahṛśā. 6.49-59)*

Auspicious Scenes In Dream:

If a person sees *devas* (gods), *dvijas* (brahmins); cows, bulls, alive friends, kings, saints, praiseworthy persons, ablaze fire, clean water reserver, fair complexioned lady with white cloth, bright childrens in his dream then these symbols are to be treated as the indications of good future. Again, in dream if he (the dreamer) sees that he is surrounded by the *rākṣasas* whose bodies are smeared with blood and for that they are looking brightful then this symbol also presays something auspicious for morrow. He who receives umbrella, mirror, white cloth with fragrance in dream gets good result in near future.

Mountain, tree full of fruits, lion, elephant, the bullock cart, a person who is crossing river or lake or ocean-all are the good symbols of auspices in dream.

He who moves from east to north in dream as a result of this he may be endowed with long span of life and wealth.

(Ahṛśā. 6. 62-71).[1]

1. *Āyurvediya Mahākoṣa*,pp. 1685-'87.

IV. 2 METAPHYSICS OF DREAM

IV. 2.0. EPISTEMOLOGY OF DREAM-KNOWLEDGE

When mind is associated with a specific region *(i.e. pradeśaviśeṣa)* of a nerve, called *medhyā*, at that time dream takes place. Here, the author Nilakaṇṭha further clarifies what that specific region means. He says: the specific region means the junction of the Puritat vein *(Puritat nāḍi)* and the external region or it may be conceived as region in one's own self, where external sensory-organs donot exist.[1]

As *saṁskāra* (impression) causes *smṛti* (remembrance) so also *svapnajñāna* is caused by *saṁskāra*. In other words, the mental-perception generated by *saṁskāra* is called *svapnajñāna*. So saṁskāra is at the root of both smṛti and *svapnajñāna*. When the *ā tman* (the soul) gets connected with *manas* (the mind) in a specific way it yields a special type of mental knowledge which is otherwise known as *svapna*. Here, the relation is of special type between *medhyānāḍi* and mind. The effect of this relation is illusory-knowledge. Here, by the word *pūrvānubhava* the author wants to mean the past experience, either of this life or of previous life.[2]

Svapnajñāna (the dream-knowledge) is created out of bodily humours *(doṣas)* or specific thoughts *(cintā-viśeṣa)* or something unknown and unseen special type of experience. This knowledge is possible only when mind is in the same phase of time where the *puritatnāḍi* and the external region come together. This knowledge is included into a category of *mānasviparyaya* (i.e. the mental illusion).[3] When the sense-faculties are withdrawn and mind gets dissolved in that state of mind (i.e. the *pralinamanaska* state) the reproduction of the sensual experience by mind is called *svapna* (the dream). This is a mental phenomenon. By this way the knowledge of dream is produced.

In the *pralina*-state (of the mind) outward sense-organs cease to function. In other words, they are incapable of apprehending any object of knowledge. At that stage due to the intensity of two winds namely, *prāṇa* (in-breathing) and *apāna* (out-breathing) and the special type of connection between *ātman* called *svāpa* and mind, *svapnajñāna* is generated. This is caused by the impressions of the objects experienced earlier. In dream mind experiences because of *saṁskāra* the non-existent (i.e. the unreal) objects in non-perceptual form.[4]

This mental perception gets generated because of *alaukika-sannikarṣa*[5] (i.e. the extra-ordinary contact).

NOTES AND REFERENCES

1. *Pradeśaviśeṣa avasthitamanaḥsaṁyogaḥ, medyā manaḥsaṁyogo vā. Atra pradeśaviśeṣastu puritat bahir deśayoh sandhiḥ Nirindriya ātmapradeśo vā cintayah.* *(Nīlakaṇṭhī Guṇagrantha. p. 38).*
2. *Smṛtau yathā saṁskāraḥ kāraṇam tathā svapna saṁjñaka mānasajñānepi ityāha tathā iti. Tathā ātmamanaḥsamyogaviśeṣāt pūrvānubhavajanita saṁskārāt ca svapno mānasajñānaviśeso bhavati. Atra saṁyoge viśeṣo medhyāmanaḥsaṁyogāt-makadoṣaviśiṣṭatvam. Ata eva tadānīm bhrama eva bhavati. Pūrvānubhavaśca aihiko janmān-tarīyo vā. (Vai. Sū Vivṛ. on sū. 9.2.7)*
3. *Svapnajñānam puritat bahirdeśayoḥsaṁdhau manasi sthite adṛṣṭaviśeṣeṇa cintāviśeṣaṇa dhātu doṣeṇa vā janyate. Tacca mānasaviparyaye antarbhavati. (Sid. Can. Guṇa chap. p. 34)*
4. *Uparate indriyagrāmasya pralīnamanaskasya indriya-dvāreṇa eva yad anubhavanam mānasam tat svapnajñā-nam. Praline ca tasmin uparate indriyagrāmo bhavati, tasyām avasthāyām prabandhena prāṇa apāna santāna pravṛttau ātma manaḥsaṁyoga viśeṣāt svāpākhyāt saṁskārācca indriyadvāreṇa eva asatsu visayeṣu pratyakṣākāram svapna-jñānam utpadhyate.*

(Praśasta. bhā pp. 436-38)

5. *Atra ca mānasam jñānam jñānalakṣaṇarūpa alaukika-sannikarṣāt bhavati.........*
(Vai. Sū. Vivṛ. 9.2.7)

IV. 2.1. PHILOSOPHY OF DREAM

Coming to the *Upaniṣadic* literature (600 B.C.)* we find that in the *Kaṭha. Upa.* the word *svapna* has occurred once, in the *Praśna. Upa.* thrice, in the *Māṇḍū. Upa* thrice, in the *Aita. Upa* once, in the *Chā. Upa.* four times, in the Bṛ. Upa eight times, in the *Mai. Upa* once and in the Śrīmad. Gītā. once.

Apart from the occurence in the Śrīmad. Gītā, where the word *svapna* mostly means 'sleep' and the occurrence in the *Ait. Upa.* where it denotes three meanings namely, *Jāgrat, Svapna and Suṣupti* elsewhere the word occurs in the respective Upas. in the sense of 'dream'. A cursory glance at the following places will substantiate our observation.

Kaṭha. Upa. 2.3.5

Praśna. Upa. 4.1. 5,6.

Māṇḍū. Upa. 4,5, 10.

Ait. Upa. 3.12

Chā. Upa. 5.2.8, 8,6.3, 8.10.1 & 8.11.1.

Bṛ. Upa. 4.3.7, 11, 13, 15, 16, 17, 18 & 19.

Mai. Upa. 4.2

Śrimad. Gītā 18

In the minor *Upas.* like Mahopaniṣad (Mahā. Upa.), Śārīrakopaniṣad (Śārī. Upa), Yogaśikhopaniṣad (Yoga. Upa). etc also we notice a host of references regarding svapna. These minor Upas too use the word in any of the three senses namely, sleep, dream and deep sleep. The *Mahā. Upa.* goes to define *svapna* as follows.

"Alpakālam mayā dṛṣṭam etad na udeti yatra hi.

Parāmarśaḥprabuddhasya sa svapna iti kathyate."
(Mahā. Upa. 5.16)

The meaning of this verse is "Dream is that which is experienced only for a short time and is revived after awakening that such an experience doesnot apparently arise anywhere."[2]

We do not find any description regarding how dream is created in the *Upas.* But at the later stage we get an elaborate discussion how dream objects are created in the *Māṇḍū Upa. kārikās of Gauḍapāda.* It may be noticed that the *Upas.* start philosophising dream. It has been philosophised first in the Śat. Brā. where it is said that being identified with the self, *svapna* goes from this world to the next world.[3]

This trend went on a bit developing in course of time in the Bṛ Upa. also belonging to the same Brā. The same verse of Śat. Brā. 14.7.1.7 is attested in this *Upa.* Some other mantras of this *Upa* also describe philosophical value of *svapna.*

For example, verse no. 4.3.11. states that in the dream state, self being akin with dream keeps its body aside and moves around in order to have a vision about those who are asleep.

Mantra no. 4.3.15 refers to the enjoyment of that self in the *svapna* state before it transcends to the *suṣupti* state. *Mantra* no. 4.3.16 also reiterates about the existence of the same self in the *suṣupti* state, which is termed as *samprasāda,* because of its highest serenity. Next *mantra* (4.3.19) talks about the absence of the dream-knowledge in this state. Because, in this state no desire remains. So no dream-knowledge is possible. The *Praśna Upa.* observes that since the mind is overpowered by *tejas,* no desire arises. So no dream takes place in *suṣupti* state.[4]

Again, the reference of *Ait Upa.* points out the three abode of self by saying that *'Tasya traya āvasathāḥ trayaḥ svapnā.... (Ait. Upa. 3.12).* Here, the word *svapna* denotes all the three meanings. Now, the question arises in dream-state all external sense organs stop functioning so by which means do we get knowledge? The answer follows from the reference of the *Praśna. Upa. Mantra No. 4.5* deals with the epistemology of dream-knowledge. It says that in dreamstate mind alone works, through which we have dream-knowledge. Again, question may be raised what for the Advaitins have started philosophising dream? The answer is, according to them non-dual self alone is real. So in order to falsify the external reality of the world they have taken dream as a simile. Because, it's a wellknown fact that the objects shown in the knowledge of dream are unreal. And hence, the knowledge gets sublated after the dreamer gets up. *Mantra* No. 4.10 of Yogo Upa. speaks in the same tone. True knowledge is that which remains as it is all through, where *bādhakajñāna* never arises. But on the contrary, the knowledge which is immediately followed by a *bādhakajñāna* is a false knowledge which always happens in the case of dream-knowledge.

Māṇḍu. Upa. states about the four-fold division of the consciousness (i.e. the self). This upa. also defines each state minutely.* The simple reason behind this classification is they want to nullify the reality of the whole world in a comparative and contrastive way. In comparison to the awakened state, dream-state is unreal. And from *turīya* (the highest reality) point of view all are unreal.

As an Advaitin Gauḍapāda has tried to deny the reality of the awakening-state on the basis of the simile of the dream-knowledge. According to him, the knowledge acquired in the dream-state and the knowledge acquired in the awakened-state both are on par.

The logic forwarded by him in his *kārikās (kās)* are as follows: Wise persons say that the dream related to any object, which exists externally is unreal, unsubstantial. Because, the root of all these objects are *antaḥstha* (internal). All *bhāvas* (entities) are covered internally. External entities donot have reality because they are projected out of *bhāvas* existing inside. In short, external entities are the projections of the internals. The projection itself is individual's mental activity. And hence, projection is *vitatha* (false).[5] Things which appear in dream are not real, because of *antaḥsaṁvṛtatva.* There is no space to accommodate an elephant, which may appear in dream.

In dream place and time do not substantiate their reality. And whosoever dreams after getting up from that state he realises that he was dreaming.[6]

We can support this very fact by quoting reference from the *Śruti,* where it has been mentioned about the non-existence of rathadi etc.* After getting up it becomes obvious that the knowledge of a chariot in dream was false. Because, at present that entity doesnot exist. Here the unsubstantial nature of dream is indicated.[7] Now, Gauḍpāda tries to falsify both the states. According to him *Jāgrat* is also *vitatha* on the same basis. Here, he wants to mean *Jāgrat* and *svapna* both are one and the same. *Smṛti* confirms this fact. Dream objects are located in the *antaḥkaraṇa.* Internal perception is covered by *antaḥkaraṇacatuṣtaya . (i.e. manas, buddhi, citta and ahaṁkāra).* Since the external objects are the projection of internal ones both are equally unreal.[8]

Since *bhāvapadārthas* (entities), which appear in dream do not exist either in the beginning or at the end, therefore, their *saprayojanatā* etc. get contradicted in the dream-state. So they should be regarded as false one *(vitatha).*[9]

Gauḍapāda points out the differentiation of the objects in both the states. In dream things may appear which have not been experienced earlier (in the *jāgrata* state). This is the characteristic of the localized self *(Jīvātman),* which is termed as *sthānin,* who goes and looks at them (objects). This is the property of the seer but not of the one who is being perceived. So it becomes subjective.[10] Even as regards the *svapnavṛtti,* it has been conceived by internal consciousness *(antaścetas).* So it is unreal. If it is apprehended by exteriorised consciousness then this seems to be real but in reality both are unreal.[11]

In the awakened state also if objects are conceived by internal consciousness these have to be *asat*. If it is argued that the objects are known by external consciousness then it is obvious that both are unreal.[12]

Both the states are unreal though they differ in place. One is external and the other one is internal. Now, the question arises who would cognize all these illusory entities? The answer is it is he who finds out that difference between the differentiator and the differentiated.[13]

Coming to this stage we notice an elaborate discussion about the creation of the objects in both the states. The author says that because of his *māyā* the god creates everything through himself. He himself is *kartṛ* and *karaṇa*. *Māyā* is also treated here as an instrument or the strength applied to the instrument. *Ātman* himself understands the differentiation of creation that the *Jagrat, svapna and suṣupti* are the vikalpa of *turīya*.[14]

According to the Vedāntins the whole world is like a *gandharvanagar* which appears in a dream.[15] Both *bhāvas and asadbhāvas* are created by *advaya* (non-dual). *Dvaya* is the creation of all *asadbhāvas*. In other words, *asadbhāvas (gandharvanagar etc.)* are the creation of duality. Duality seems to exist in the world which is created by the *asadbhāvas*. Existing *bhāvas* point out non-duality in comparison to *asadbhāvas*. In short, *bhāvas of jagrat are sadbhā vas and bhāvas of svapna are asadbhāvas*. Since both the state are on par, both can lead to *advaya*, which alone is highest truth.[16]

Māyā starts vibrating, mind creates through *māyā* the image of duality in *svapna*. Likewise, the duality in the awakening state is also the creation through mind by *māyā*.[17] To be more clear, mind creates both duality and non-duality in dream. Likewise, both are created by mind in the awakened-state also. So whatever is created by mind through *māyā* is unreal. *Advaya and Dvaya* both are *ābhā sas*. Both of these are caused by *manas* through *māya* and not by *ā tman*. In short, the unity of lower level and the duality of the lower level both are mental creation through *māyā*. The highest one without second is realized in the *turīya* state through *ātman* but not by *māyā*. Therefore, in that state there will be no *māyin*.[18]

Duality is mental perception. When this mind gets dissolved or it leads to beyond the level of mind i.e. the non-mental state and in that stage duality ceases to exist. Duality is not at all found there, which may be compared with *māyā*.[19] When mind is overpowered completely, non-conceivable, rational, such kind of state of cognition is different from *suṣupti* and this state is not equal to any other state. According to the Advaitins this state (i.e. *turīya* state) is alone true.[20] In the *suṣupti* state mind gets dissolved. But if it is *nigṛhīta* then it doesnot get dissolved. For the time being it is dissolved, as in the case of sugar mixed in water. Here when water is dried up then sugar alone remains. But if it is transcended by *cittavṛttinirodha* then that state will be known as *turīya*, where there will be no fear. That is the illumined state because of *ātmajñāna*. In comparison to that, *suṣupti* is full of darkness.[21]

In that state everything namely, the birth cycle, sleep, dream, nā marūpa etc. cease to exist.[22]

In *svapna* nothing is objective *(avastuka)* unsubstantial. Because, the condition of the body doesnot fit with the visible-objects. Since in dream all are perceived mentally not by physical eyes.[23]

The author of the *Mā.kā.* endeavours to falsify Jāgrata-state in a reverse way by pointing out that the objects of the awakening state are unreal.

He says that *svapna* has its root or seed in the *jāgrata* state. [24] *Praśana. Upa.* also corroborates this fact.[25] What does not exist in *jāgarita* state a person sees even that in dream when he becomes one with that. *Rajju* of the awakened-state appears as serpent in dream-state. *Rajju* is sat in the awakened-state. But when it appears as *sarpa* then it becomes *asat*, because of its non-existence. In the awakened-state *sarpa* is *asat* in comparison to *Rajju*. But it becomes sat in the dreamstate. Non-existence of a thing becomes existent in *svapna* state. To be more clear, '*asat* is seen in *jāgarita*' means I have seen *sarpa* in place of *rajju*. So awakening state before *svapna is asat*, awakening state after *svapna is also asat*. In between of the two, the *svapna* state is also *asat* because of its momentarily appearance *(Pratibuddho na paśyati)*[26] *Yoga. Upa.* has the similar observation.[27]

As there is erroneous knowledge in the awakened-state so also in the dream-state. Naturally, no distinction can be maintained.[28] In dreamstate the non-dual and dual both are seen by the *citta*. Likewise, the duality and non-duality experiences in the awakened-state are because of *citta*, which is overpowered by *māyā*.[29]

Through all these arguments Gauḍapāda tried to show that as the objects of the knowledge of dream state are unreal, so also those of the awakened state.

NOTES & REFERENCES

**Ghatage, A. M.(ed)* An Encyclopaedic Dictionary of Sanskrit on Historical Principles, Vol. 1, p. LXXIII.

2. Swain, B.K., Philosophy of the Mahopaniṣad.
3. Śat. Brā 14.7.1.7.
4. Praśna. Upa. 4.6

* (i) Jāgaritasthāno bahiṣprajñaḥ saptāṅga ekonaviṁśati-mukhaḥ sthūlabhuk vaiśvānaraḥ prathamaḥ pādaḥ. (Māṇḍū Upa. 3)

(ii) Svapnasthāno 'ntaprajñaḥ saptāṅga ekonaviṁśati mukhaḥ praviviktabhuk taijaso dvitīyaḥ pādaḥ (Māṇḍū Upa.4)

(iii) Yatra supto na kaṁcana kāmam kāmayate na kaṁcana svapnam paśyati tat suṣuptam.
Suṣuptasthāna ekībhūtaḥ prajñānaghana eva 'nanda-mayo hi ānandabhukta cetomukhaḥ prājñāstṛtī

yaḥ pādaḥ (Māṇḍū. Upa. 5)

(iv) Nāntaḥprajñam na bahiṣprajñam na ubhayataḥ-prajñam na prajñānaghanam na prajñam na aprajñam. Adṛṣṭam avyavahāryam agrāhyam alakṣaṇam acintyam avyapadeśyam ekātmapratyaya-sāram prapañcopaśamam śāntam śivam advaitam caturtham manyante.

5. Vaitathyam sarvabhāvānām svapna āhur manīṣiṇaḥ Antaḥsthānāttu bhāvānām saṁvṛtatvena hetunā. (Mā Kā. 2/1)

6. Adīrghatvacca kālasya gatvā deśānna paśyati. Pratibuddhaśca vai sarvastasmin deśe na vidyate. (Mā Kā. 2/2)

* Bṛ. Upa. 4.3.10.

7. Abhāvaśca rathādīnām śruyate nyāyapūrvakam. Vaitathyam tena vai prāptam svapna āhuḥ prakāśitam. (Mā kā. 2/3)

8. Antaḥsthānāttu bhedānām tasmājjāgarite smṛtam. Yathā tatra tathā svapne saṁvṛtatvena bhidyate (Mā kā. 2/4)

9. Saprayojanatā teṣāṁ svapne vipratipadyate. Tasmād ādyantavattvena mithyā eva khalu te smṛtāḥ (Mā kā. 2/8)

10. Apūrvam sthānidharmo hi yathā svarganivāsinām. Tānayam prekṣate gatvā yathā eva iha suśikṣitah. (Mā. kā 2/8)

11. Svapnavṛttāvapi tu antaścetasā kalpitam tu asat. Bahiścetogṛhītam sad dṛṣtam vaitathyametayoḥ (Mā kā. 2/9)

12. Jagratvṛttau api tu antaścetasā kalpitam tu asat. Bahiścetogṛhitam sad yuktam vaitathyametayoh. (Mā kā 2/10)

13. Ubhayorapi vaitathyam bhedānām sthānayor yodi. Ka etān budhyate bhedān ko vai teṣām vikalpakaḥ(Mā Kā. 2/11)

14. Kalpayati ātmanā ātmānām ātmā devaḥ svamāyayā. Sa eva budhyate bhedān iti Vedāntaniścayaḥ(Mā Kā. 2/12)

15. Svapnamāye yathā dṛṣṭe gandharvanagaram.

Tathā viśvamidam dṛṣṭam vedānteṣu vicakṣanaih.
(Mā kā. 2/31).

16. Bhāvair asadbhir eva ayam advayena ca kalpitaḥ. Bhāva api advayena eva tasmād dvayatā sivā. (Mā kā. 2/33)
17. Yathā svapne dvayābhāsam spandate māyayā manaḥ Tathā jāgrat dvayābhāsam spandate māyayā manaḥ(Mā Kā 3/29)
18. Advayam ca dvayābhāsam manaḥ svapne na saṁśayaḥ (Mā kā. 3/30)
19. Manodṛśyam idam dvaitam yatkiṁcit sacarācaram. Manaso hi amanībhāve dvaitam na eva upalabhyate. (Mā kā. 3/31)
20. Nigṛhītasya manaso nirvikalpasya dhīmataḥ. Pracāraḥ sa tu vijñeyaḥ suṣupte 'nyo na tatsama. (Mā Kā. 3/34)
21. Liyate hi suṣupte tannigṛhītam na līyate. Tadeva nirbhayam brahma jñānālokam samantataḥ(Mā Kā. 3/35)
22. Ajama anidram asvapnam anāmakam arupakam (Mā Kā. 3/35)
23. Svapne ca avastukaḥ kāyaḥ pṛthaganyasya darśanāt. Yathā kāyastathā sarvam cittadṛsyam avastukam (Mā Kā. 4/36)
24. Grahaṇād Jāgaritavad tad hetuḥ svapna isyate. (Mā Kā. 4/37)
25. Praśna Upa. 4.5
26. Asad jāgarite dṛstvā svapne paśyati tadmayaḥ Asat svapne 'pi dṛṣṭvā ca pratibuddho na paśyati. (Mā Kā. 4/39)
27. Yoga. Upa. 4.10
28. Viparyāsād yathā Jāgrad acintyān bhūtavatspṛśet. Tathā svapne viparyāsāddharmāḥ tatraiva paśyati. (Mā Kā. 4/41)
29. Yathā svapne dvayābhāsam cittam calati māyayā. Tathā jāgrad dvayābhāsam cittam calati māyayā. (Mā Kā. 4/61)

CHAPTER - V

WESTERN TRADITION

V.0 ANATOMY AND PHYSIOLOGY OF DREAM.

Dream is a psychic phenomenon which occurs during sleep. Now, a question may be raised what does sleep achieve for human being? In Shakespeare's words sleep plays the role of chief nourishment. To Shakespeare's Macbeth, however, sleep was 'sore labour's bath, balm of hurt minds, great nature's second course, chief nourisher in lifes feasts'.

Naturally sleep restores the body after labour. Restoration of a building, which is inert can be possible by using old materials, but in case of living being it is quite impossible. Only by the process of restoration living cells are reinspired or reenriched for proper functioning. So sleep of living creature is a required factor. And in this way of synthesis sleep plays an important role.[1]

As Thomas Dekker has defined sleep by saying that "Sleep is the golden chain that which ties health and our bodies together."[2]

Sleep is of two types: Paradoxical sleep and Orthodox sleep. Paradoxical sleep is that sleep where Rapid Eye Movements (REMS) take place. And just vice-versa is called orthodox sleep i.e. where there is no REM. This is the non-REM state of the sleeper. By adopting some laboratory investigation it is learnt that the throat muscle thrilling is the first symbol of the REM.[3]

Now, after getting this conception one learner may be curious to know that in which sleep dream occurs? Whether in either of these two or in one sleep out of these two?

While answering in his book, entitled 'sleep', when do we dream? Ian oswald says "At the time of writing the general opinion would, I think, be that vivid, adventurous dreams are most often contemporary with rapid eye movement periods, but that dreams no less vivid and adventurous are sometimes experienced when first asleep and mental life during sleep is by no means confined to rapid-eye-movement periods but can occur at any time of the night".[4]

Since modern Psychology has divided sleep into two categories and hence, from the statement of Ian Oswald we may conclude that in both the states of sleep dream occurs i.e., in REM as well as in non-REM period.

A claim was made that dreaming will not take place if a person undergoes a brain operation, which is called modified leucotomy. But after that operation also it has been observed that critical REMS take place. What is new is this that a leucotomized patient doesn't bother to remember the dreamt-event. But sometimes he asserts that he was dreaming.[5]

In paradoxical sleep all muscles are not paralysed because throughout sleep we breathe. But most of the muscles are not only paralysed but simply cease to function, e.g. the twitch of the leg muscle, which in the awakened-state and in the orthodoxsleep involuntarily carries a nerve stimuli from sense-organs to the spinal cord.[6]

The paralysis of some parts of the body is momentary but it occurs frequently. Any part of the body movement is related to certain dream-action in a paradoxical sleep. Nerve impulses climb down to the spinal cord to generate the paralysis and stop the nerve cells there from firing off the messages, which brings muscle into action. These descending impulses are suddenly intensified with each burst of REMS. The twitches of the limbs are usually accompanied by every burst of REM. After examining a group of people (middle aged Edinburg citizens) investigators arrived at a conclusion that major body-movements take place in every minute twice as frequent during paradoxical sleep as during orthodox sleep. Because of the greater restlessness in that sort of sleep attempt has been made to call that sleep as 'light sleep'. Some psychologists have tried to identify paradoxical-sleep as 'light sleep' tentatively. They have putforth an example of a cat. In the cat the electrical firing off cells of the cerebral cortex is much reduced in orthodox-sleep in comparison to the awakened-state. On the otherhand, in a paradoxical-sleep, the firing rates remain intact, as in the case of wakeful state, but the rhythmic patterns get changed and they are not well-arranged. This sort of similarity might have tempted them to designate paradoxical sleep as 'light sleep'. If we emphasize on pattern changing then we won't be able to include it in the paradoxical sleep category. So the safer way to think of that sleep as different in kind rather than arranging it in some sort of hierarchy.[7]

Some people say they dream everynight for few minutes. Some say they donot dream at all. But Psychologists discovered that, by using alarm clock if a sleeper gets up from sleep, he will report that he was dreaming. Sleep prohibits to form a clear memory. This is the reason for which we forget everything about dreamt-event.

Very often dreams are defined as a succession of visual images or mental picutres. But Ian Oswald disagreed on this point. He says "when people say, I saw a huge bus coming towards me in a dream. It was not just a moving picture of a bus. It was experienced as something having a vivid personal reference, coming towards me, in a situation where the 'me' was then not in real time but in dream-time. In reality I was in bed. But I was experiencing the adventure of an unreal life, a dreamlife, in which I was far removed from my downy pillow." According to him dream is a part of fantasy. He further holds that even a born-blind dreams, though he doesnot have the conception of what seeing is? Just as in real life he meets people, hears things, feels things, smells things, so all these appear in dream. But he doesnot see things. This is corroborated by a laboratary investigation.

A drowsy person settles in bed for sleep; the quality of his mental life changed, contact with reality gradually became more and more weaker, when someone made him wake up, at that time, he reported about dreaming. His daydreams merged into night dreams. This was the outcome of the investigation by using Electro-Encephalograph (EEG). In this stage EEG lost its alpha rhytham and a pattern of low voltage slow waves were present. Normal people dream much later in the night. At that time the appearance of the EEG will be drowsy.

In Chicago, in the year 1950, Dr. Kleitman and Dr. Aserinsky were studying the sleep of infants, when they were one month old. Investigators observed that every hours a recurrent or cyclical pattern of restlessness, the infants eyes moved about for a few minutes under the closed eye-lids. The similar periodic change in sleep is also found in adults by using EEG machine. Instead of an hourly periodicity, in case of adults they assigned one and half-hours. After investigation they reached to a conclusion that near about 80% dreams had been reported after getting up from REMS but only 7% by other than REM awakenings. These 7% were remembered only fragmentarily unlike the narrative dreams of the REM periods. The conclusion was each night several times dreams occur though we don't remember after getting up from that.

Without consenting the theory of the researcher of Chicago a team of research workers in New York, in order to get it confirmed, again tried to probe into this matter. They selected one group of those, who said they were frequent dreamers and a second group of those, who thought they never dreamt. After getting up from sleep, sometimes from period of sleep with motionless eyes and sometimes from REM periods, the dreamers reported dreams after 53% and 93% of these awakenings respectively, the non-dreamers after 17% and 46% respectively. The experimenters had also found the same sort of cyclical pattern in all night sleep as the Chicago workers. Being thoroughly convinced, the Newyorkers proposed that "The fairly high incidence of dream reports from sleep with motionless eyes could well be attributed to recall of what had been dreamt in a prior REM period."

The most important point which was stressed by those experimenters was that those who designate themselves as non-dreamer, the simple reason behind this for them dream is quite bizarre or crazy. People seem they forget dreamt-event at once. But actually they don't give much importance to dreaming. Being asked by somebody a non-dreamer might say, he had not been dreaming, he was thinking. They think that dream consists of some bizarre elements.

Further investigation shows clearly the rapidity of REM due to which dreams will be forgotten. This investigation reveals that after getting up from REM dreamer will be able to describe his dream fully. But if a person gets up after five or ten minutes when a REM is over, he will hardly recall the dreamt event. He cannot remember in detail. Variations in frequency of dream recall involves so many aspects of the dreamer viz. remembering capacity, motivation, intellect and co-operation.[8]

Person, gets up from non-REM state very often reports that he was thinking about the events of the previous day.[9] The determined method about the dream acitivity and its relation to psychological variations during sleep as Aserinsky and Kleitman reported after a regorous testing of the relation between eye-movement and simultaneous occurence of dream. The knowledge of the dream is the subjective report of the dream. But by applying this method i.e. recording the REMS through EEG it becomes relatively objective one. This type of investigation is a contrast of subjective with the objective recall of dreams. In subjective forgetting, distortion etc. take place. Thus by applying this process of investigation it has become possible to study objectively the effect on dreaming of environmental changes, psychological stress, drug administration and a variety of other factors and influences.[10]

The results of these experiments reveal that "Dreaming accompanied by REMS and a low-voltage EEG occured periodically in discrete episodes during the course of night sleep."[11] Of course, it cannot be said firmly that, exclusively in REM periods dream occurs and in non-REM state dream doesn't occur. As a matter of fact, the brain waves are at the lightest level of sleep only during REM period and very high level at other times. In non-REMS period which dream occurs generally we don't remember because the dream which had occured in REM state persists unusually long time. This is carried out by the fact that most of these dreams occur very closely, within eight minutes, at the end of the REM period.[12] Some other workers group themselves to reckon dreaming as the pysiological phenomena. According to them dream is the outcome of bodily disorder. Among the investigators Wada pointed out that dreaming and gastric contractions are simultaneous. Of course, this conclusion was partial because on the basis of only seven awakenings in two Ss* he drew this conclusion. And that too, out of these two one was unable to recall the content though he felt he was dreaming. The other one recollects the content of the dreamknowledge thrice out of four awakenings.

Further attempt has been made by Scantlebury, Frick and Patterson to study the dreaming and its relation to gastric activity. On the basis of three examples of dream recall out of seven awakenings, they deduce judiciously "The exact time during which a dream occurs is elusive of record." So from the above discussion we may conclude that the investigators have failed to conclusively decide whether the dream occurs due to gastric disorder.

Another researcher, McGlade held this view that if the foot twitches occur after the onset of sleep that will cause dreaming. He took a series of foot twitches in order to postulate the simultaneity of these two fact viz., the occurrence of dream and the beginning of foot twitches are invariably related with each other. But the postulation was not correct. Because, in the course of investigation foot twitches didnot take place in all cases of the 25 Ss, chosen for experiment. Out of 25 Ss three only exhibited their foot twitches. Other painstaking effort was made for the incidental observation of dreaming by studying brain waves. Investigators tried their best to fix up a link between brain waves and the occurrence of dream. To them dream has co-incidental base. But they failed to finger out anything specifically. They concluded that all sorts of brain waves are relevant to dreaming. They did not mention anything about the actual recollection of the dreamt content.[13]

In other study of dreaming, attempt has been made to localize dream activity. It was found that dreams, during the night, might be recalled at any time, but most of the dreams were recalled by the dreamers in the later part of sleep. This was tested by awakening Ss at different times of sleep period.[14]

As Ian Oswald, the author of the book entitled "Sleep" believes some sort of mental life goes on throughout the night though it is almost forgotten. But it gets special importance during the time when REM occurs simultaneously. This quality is found in dreaming.[15] Dream doesnot occur momentarily or with great rapidity as people think about it. It seemed to progress at a proportional rate in comparison to a real experience of the same. It has been observed that if the period of REMS are increased or enhanced then the length of dream will also invariably be increased. This would not have happened if dreams were instantaneous. And hence, any length of REM period be easily accomodated by infinite number of dream activity.[16]

On the basis of experiment it was found that "the periods of REMS and dreaming and the regularity with which they occur are an intrinsic part of normal sleep."[17]

Kleitman and his Co-workers stated that the REMS are nothing but looking at the dream-picture-movements. In REMS period facial twitches also occur in human beings. Now question is, do they occur simultaneously or the expression of total condition of the nervous system which prevails during these times irrespective of accompanying mental life?

The American workers looked at their Electrical Records (ERS) of the moments just before awakening and noted down the last direction of the last eye movement in each case, whomsoever they have tested. They started asking the dreamer about the last event of the dream and anticipated the last probable direction of eyemovement that would have accompanied such an event in real life. There was a remarkable close concordance between these directions.

The Chicago workers also went through the electrical records of the dreams by dividing each eyemovement period as 'active' and 'passive' depending on the profusion of the eyemovements and reported that these are related to the nature of the dream-content. To watch a lawn tennis in reality requires more eye-movements than the watching Television. The same thing if happens in dream the earlier one would be 'active' and the later one is 'passive'.

Those who disagreed on this view underwent further investigation by taking up some ERS of 'active' and 'passive' dreams. A final and deciding judgment was made eventually by giving every record a consistant score twice out of three times.

Again Ralph Berger carried out experiments with full precautions, no concordance showed up to strengthen the looking at the dreampictures theory. But as per the explanation of Ian Oswald, something happens in the brain for several moments before the eyemovement starts. If we posit the eyemovements as looking responses of the dream-events and dream occurs continuously rather than a sudden flash then it would be difficult to explain the brain-wave sequence before eyemovement.

If the brain waves simply indicate a recurrent change in the electrical status quo of the brain then the eyemovements can be visualized as sequel.

In order to deny the looking at the dream pciture theory by investigating some blind men Ian Oswald says, blind perons, who does not see in his dream, probably still gets REM. But these can never be treated as looking-at-the-dream picture movements. Similarly a newborn baby also gets eye-movements in sleep. But we cannot expect from him to organise a dream life, full of visual incidents. Because at that state he doesnot have that much strong memory to build it up. He concludes that the eyemovements are not looking-at-the dream moments but are the symbols of the brain excitement and that lavish eye-movements are the mark of high brain excitement, reproduced in exciting dreams.[18]

One may also be sure about this fact that one dreams at any assigned time provided some stimuli are applied from outside. As Chicago workers tried to corroborate this fact by aiding light flashes, musical notes and water sprinkling. After getting up from their dream they related about their dreamt-event. It was found that whatever they described that related to outside stimuli. Whosoever dreamt of a lake or pond, water spray was the aiding stimulus in his case. So it is understood that the outside stimuli are capable enough to provoke the same type of content of dream-knowledge. Sometime calling bell or telephone ring is also incorporated into the dreamlife.[19]

NOTES & REFERENCES

1. Oswald, Ian, *Sleep*, pp. 143
2. Ibid, pp. 152
3. Ibid, pp. 100
4. Ibid, pp. 69
5. Ibid, pp. 69.
6. Ibid, pp. 100.
7. Ibid, pp. 100-102
8. Ibid, pp. 64-69
9. Ibid, pp. 72
10. Dement, William & Kleitman, Nathaniel, "The Relation of Eye Movements During Sleep to Dream Activity", pp. 345-46
11. Ibid, pp. 345
12. Ibid, pp. 345

*Ss. = Subjects of the experiment.

13. Ibid, pp. 345.
14. Ibid, p. 345.
15. *Sleep,* op. cit. pp. 73
16. Dement, William & op. cit, p. 346
17. Ibid, pp. 345
18. Oswald, Ian, op. cit. pp. 73-79
19. Ibid, p. 80.

V.0.1. THE MATERIALS AND SOURCES OF DREAMS

Freud held the view that in every dream we have some sort of experience of the preceding day. Almost all dreams refer to the previous day's incident as its content. But Havelock Ellis holds a different opinion. He does not believe in such periodical reproduction of dreams. He pointed out some lacuna in the impressions of the immediate past. According to him "The dream may select its material from any period of life, provided only that a chain of thought leads back from the experience of the day of the dream (the recent impressions) of that earlier period."[1] The stimulus of the dream-formation may be objective experience, which has been made current by the mental activity of the day; this view is held by Freud. He has chalked out the various stipulations under which dream sources are operative. He says that the sources of the dream may be as follows:

(i) A fact which is recent and psychologically important may directly be represented in dream.

(ii) Several recent and significant events may be jotted down by dream into a unified-whole.

(iii) One or more than one current and significant contemporary events may be reproduced in dream content indirectly.

(iv) An experience (recollections or a chain of thought) which has subjective importance, which is constantly represented in the dream by allusion to a recent but indifferent impression. Further he holds that an event which is psychologically significant but not recent may be replaced for the purpose of dream formation by a recent but psychologically indifferent event if that event satisfies the following criteria.

(a) The dream content has to keep a connection with things recently apprehended.

(b) The dream stimulus should be a psychologically significant event.

Indifferent impressions may also form dream provided these are of recent origin. But sometimes the earlier impressions of our lives also appear in dream. If it were the criterion regarding the formation of the dream that only recent impressions will occur in dream then how does it happen in dream that some earlier impressions also form dream content? There is no such hard and fast rule regarding the sources of dream. The event may belong to either earlier life (which has already passed) or present life, it may appear in dream provided it is an event of psychological importance. As strümpell puts it "No psychic value, and which, therefore, ought to have been forgotten long ago; elements, that is, which are neither fresh nor psychologically significant?" Due to the process of shifting and rearrangement, the replacement of the psychic significant material by another material which is altogether insiginificant and which took place in the earlier days of life gets settled in memory strongly causes dream. Only those elements which were originally indifferent are in fact no longer so, because they have acquired the value of psychologically significant material. That which has remained actually indifferent can never be reproduced in dream. From this sort of experience Freud has ascertained the following: "There are no indifferent dreamstimuli and therefore no guileless dreams. This I absolutely and unconditionally believe to be the case, apart from the dream of children, and perhaps the brief dream reactions to nocturnal-sensations. Apart from these exceptions, whatever one dreams is either plainly recognizable as being physically significant or it is distorted and can be judged correctly only after complete interpretation, when it proves after all to be psychic singificance". Dreams, which are cunning by nature also appear apparently and reveal their character as contrary or quite opposite, if one interprets it minutely says Freud.

Freud holds this view that the infantile experience may act as source for dream-formation. Except Robert all other Writers have expressed their concern over this issue. But how frequently this type of dream occurs, they couldn't decide. Because, it has happened several times that after getting up from dream the elements of that dreamt-content were not realized. So we have to deduce hereby that the childhood impressions may help generate dream. Only rare examples corroborate this fact.

If we say dreams are perennial, then sometimes sights occuring in dream in the early childhood of the dreamer may appear in dream frequently in the adult years. Freud says that if we go on interpreting dream deeply very often we will come to the track of childish experiences, which act as a source in the latent dream content. Very rarely dream reproduces its memory unchanged in the manifest dream content. As a rule Freud holds this view that an event from childhood days is represented in manifest dreamcontent as an illusion and if at all this thing happened then that illusion must be unscrewed by interpretation. By this, illusory notion may be removed. And that depends upon the efficiency of the interpretor.

At the end it has been concluded by Freud that "Such childish experiences recur at all in dreams is justified in psychoanalytic work by a great number of factors, which in their combined results appear to be sufficiently reliable. But when, for the purposes of dream interpretation, such references to childish experiences are tornout of their context, they may not perhaps seen very impressive, especially where I donot even give all the material upon which the interpretation is based."[12] Sometimes due to indigestion, dream occurs. So we may say stomach is also one of the source to form dream. Somatic stimuli plays an important role in the formation of dream. This is of three types:

(i) Because of the inner states of excitation of the sense organs, dream takes place very often. Of course, this has only subjective reality.

(ii) The objective sensory stimulus which gets generated from external objects, may cause dreaming.

(iii) The bodily stimulus which is being originated with in the body, sometimes responsible for dreaming.

Writers on dreams have flexed their brain in order to get it confirmed whether a particular psychic source may operate simultaneously with somatic stimulus or without them, altogether. In an investigation it was the outcome that "The significance of the objective excitation or the sensory organs-whether accidental stimuli operating during sleep or such as cannot be excluded from the dormant relation of these dream images and ideas to the internal bodily stimuli and confirmed by experiment; that the part played by the subjective sensory stimuli appear to be demonstrated by the recurrence of hypnogogic sensory images in dreams; and that, although the broadly accepted relation of these dream images and ideas to the internal bodily stimuli cannot be exhaustively demonstrated, it is at all events confirmed by the well-known influence which an excited state of the digestive, urinary and sexual organs exercises upon the content of our dreams."

'Nerve stimulus' and 'bodily stimulus' are the sole and exclusive sources of dreams. And both the factors are treated as anatomical sources of dreams.[3]

But there are so many loopholes in this somatic theory. The confident of the representatives of this theory may be on its factual basis, specially with regard to the sudden and external nerve-stimuli, which may be seen without any sort of intricacy in its content. But it cann't be said firmly that in the enriched content of ideas in dreams exclusively external stimulus has been caused in its formation.

Spitta has divided dreams into two categories, nervestimulus dreams and association dreams. But it was observed that unless we trace out the connection between the somatic sources and their ideational content it remained unsatisfactory.

There are two faults which the propounder of this theory could not explain. (a) Why the nature itself of the outwards stimulus is not recognized in the dream content? (b) Why the result of reaction of the mind about the wrongly conceived stimulus is indeterminate and variable? Of course, Strümpell has tried his best to answer these questions. He says during sleep mind gets lost its connection with outer-world. At that time mind is not in a proper position to interpret correctly objective sensory stimuli. rather it gets so many information from different directions and being confused it generates illusion because of unlimited stimuli from outside. In his own words "When by an external or internal nerve-stimulus during sleep a feeling, or a complex of feelings, or any sort of psychic process arises in the mind, and is perceived by the mind, this process calls up from the mind perceptual images beloning to the sphere of the waking experiences, that is to say, earlier perception, either unembellished, or with the psychic values appertaining to them. It collects about itself, as it were, a greater or lesser number of such images, from which the impression resulting from the nervestimulus receives its psychic value. In this connection it is commonly said, as in ordinary language we say of the waking procedure, that the mind interprets in sleep the impressions of nervous stimuli. The result of this interpretation is the so called nerve-stimulus dream that is, a dream the components of which are conditioned by the fact that a nerve-stimulus produces its psychical effect in the life of the mind in accordance with the laws of reproductions."

Almost all essential points are identical of this doctrine with the statement of Wundt's that "The concepts of dreams proceed, at all events for the most part, from sensory stimuli, and especially from the stimuli of general sensation, and are therefore mostly phantastic illusions - probably only to a small extent pure memory - conception raised to the condition of hallucinations."

In order to illustrate the link between dreamt content and stimuli, by which it is produced, Strümpell has employed a good simile. He says "Although the ten fingers of a person ignorant of music where to stray over the keyboard of an instrument". The implication is that dream is not psychic phenomena, though this is originated by psychic motives, but the effect of a psysiological stimulus, whose output is in psychic symtomatology because being affected by the stimuli the apparatus are not able of any other type of expression.

Meynert too attempted by employing another famous simile of the dial where individual figures were embossed to explain obsessions.

Though this somatic dream-stimuli theory has become popular and seductive it is not easy to detect its weaker points. Because, each and every somatic stimulus has power to provoke the psychic apparatus during sleep to interpret and by forming illusions it may evoke innumerable such attempts at interpretation. Somatic-stimuli may also represent in its dream-content quite different concept, other than its origin. But the theory framed by Strümpell and Wundt won't allow any sort of purpose by which the relationship between external stimuli and the dream concept chosen to interpret can be prohibited. And hence, it cannot explain the 'peculiar choice', which the stimuli often select or include materials, other than its origin in course of their dream-production.

Other question may be raised against the theory of illusions. The anticipation about mind is this during sleep is it not capable enough to realize the objective sensory stimuli in its real form? The old psychologist Burdach refuted this assumption by saying that "We must not assume that the mind is incapable of interpreting sensory stimuli in sleeping state, rather mind is not sufficiently interested in them."

The same argument of Burdach reappeared without any distortion in the work of Lipps. They have observed the inadequacy of the theory of somatic-dream stimuli as follows:

Sometimes external stimuli may not compell someone to dream but that particular stimuli occur in dream content, the moment he starts dreaming. Pathology provides us a lot of examples where the exciting stimuli of different kinds remain ineffective during sleep, though these were powerful. Sometimes it also happens that throughout our sleep we perceive sensation. e.g. Pain stimuli but the manifestation of that particular stimuli may not be into its fabrication of a dream. It may also happen that responding the stimuli person gets up in order to avoid it. Then he will not have dream. Sometimes nerve-stimulus might cause dream but other possible reactions take place as recurrently as the reaction of dream-formation. This may never be the cause unless the inspiring cause of dreaming did not lie outside the somatic dream-sources.

Taking into account the aforementioned drawbacks in the interpretation of dreams, which are caused by somatic stimuli, writers like Scherner and Philosopher like Volkelt endeavoured to determine precisely the very nature of the psychic activities which generate many-coloured images of dreams originated from somatic stimuli. While attempting to do so first of all they pointed out the nature of the dream as a problem of psychology and the dreaming is psychic activity.

Scherner gave poetical and vivid description of the psychic peculiarities which reveal themselves while forming dream. He also hit upon the method of the mind which deals with offered data of stimuli while forming dream. According to him dream is the free activity of the phantasy, which has been freed from fetter imposed on it during day time, strives to represent symbolically the nature of the organ from which stimulus proceeds. And this is the reason that from dream-images one may infer bodily sensation, conditions of the organs, the states of the stimulation etc. But due to the lack of scientifically understandable technique of interpretation delimited the wider applicability of Scherner's theory of symbolization.[4]

NOTES AND REFERENCES

1. Freud, Sigmund, op.cit., p. 70-73
2. *The Interpretation of Dreams,* op. cit. pp. 91-100
3. *The Interpretation of Dreams,* op. cit. pp. 120-21.
4. *The Interpretation of Dreams,* op. cit. pp. 121-26.

V.1. METAPHYSICS OF DREAM

V.I.0. EPISTEMOLOGY OF DREAM PERCEPTION FROM THE POINT OF VIEW OF MEDICAL SCIENCE

Perception is an instrument to acquire knowledge. This perception is of four types, namely, Physical, Physiological, Psychological and Metaphysical. If we conceive our body as an apparatus and all organs as its componant parts then the relationship between the sensory end of the apparatus, where the outward stimuli occur and the organ of sensation, which perceives things should be meaningful. Otherwise, we may not have any knowledge. In other words, without proper link knowledge may not arise at all. But unfortunately we cannot perceive the style of functioning, simply we have to infer all those happenings. We also donot know the locus and mechanism of the centre of sensation. This is our notion in general that some sort of outside excitement goes off and on to the brain through optic nerve. But we are ignorant about the decoding system of outward stimulus into apparatus. As one conveys a lot of ignorance about the construction of the brain to its psychological phenomena. The gap between the mental awareness and the brain is designated as 'mind-brain' gap.[1]

Since we are preoccupied by our belief and the superstitious society, we never perceive things fulfledgedly. We see things partially, which appear in our knowledge. Whenever we look at a particular thing, we look by our mind and never by our eyes. Because, we had the experience about that thing beforehand. And through our experience we know that thing once again.

Perception depends upon the earlier information, which the sense-organs supply to the brain and those informations act as the substratum of perception, with its all aspect. Perception can be divided into two categories, namely, the real perception and the hallucinatory perception.[2]

When sensory cues do not befit either with our knowledge or the anticipation about the universe or each other, then we have an illusory knowledge of a thing, which appear in our knowledge at that time. Dreams and illusions, both are perceptive knowledge. Both of them include external objects, which have real existence, during their apprehension. They are not imaginary altogether. Dream knowledge is dependent on the memory traces, which is created by that particular entity, being in our knowledge beforehand. In other words, the knowledge, accumulated in memory of that thing, sometimes in the past appears in the form of dream. But illusion is an analogous knowledge. It has real objective counterpart. Under certain causal complexes we have the knowledge of a particular thing. These are operative sometimes collectively, sometimes individually. When these are disturbed by any means, one particular thing reveal as illusory one i.e. contrary knowledge will arise. These illusory notion vanishes when conditions are clear. On the other hand, dream-knowledge gets sublated when a person gets up from sleep.

Perception involves so many factors. This is modified by various humourous namely, *Sattva, Rajas,* and *Tamas.* This may also be modified by the previous state of mind, drug addiction, by hunger, satiety, motivation etc.[3]

Now question may be raised: What happens to the perception in dream-state during sleep? In sleep all sense-organs stop functioning still we narrate that. 'I dreamt a nice dream during my sleep'.

Sometimes we remember 'I slept pleasantly at night'. But how could I know this? In dream though my body was in bed, I was moving in U.S.A. We are curious enough to know in my sleep how can I have this type of knowledge? What makes it possible to perceive dream, when I was asleep. Medical Science does not have satisfactory answer - says Prof. H.S. Subramanyam, a reputed psychiatrics. In comparison to them the oriental school gives more satisfactory answer. If we apply the concept of *Sākṣin*, who observes everything very minutely and constantly in our all three states of consciousness some satisfactory answer can be had. Oriental school has divided consciousness into three states namely, *jāgrat* (awakened-state), *svapna* (dream-state) and *suṣupti* (dreamless sleep). Here the *Sākṣin* is 'Self'. Sometimes ignorance delimits its real nature. When ignorance is dispelled or vanquished, only 'self' remains in its actual form. Whatever may be the perception, it takes place because of the removal of some sort of ignorance. This ignorance split the knower from the known. Because, before looking at that entity the earlier knowledge of that was covered by ignorance. The moment it is dispelled the form of that entity appears in knowledge. So we may say that the perception is a sort of transient restoration of the lost identity in between the knower and the known. When the objective attitude is overcome and the consciousness is permitted to reveal itself, at that time only the immediate knowledge is obtained.

Modern psychiatrist may not give much importance on this issue, stated by Prof. Subramanium. But he holds this view that ancient outlook provides us different outlook, various parameter to think. He says "It is time for us to wake up and search what we already have and fathom the depths of the ocean of Hindu thought processes without any prejudices."[4]

Neurophysiological evidence shows it clearly that "Any particular perception depends on the excitation of particular cells at some point in the central nervous system". This theory has been conceived by Hebb in the year 1949. Since the time of Hebb many change has taken place in his theory. Again his main thesis requires a bit expansion where the patterns evoked in the brain are moduolated by the junctional anatomy of the synaptic and dendritic.

"Sensory percepuon and memory consolidation are composed of an initial set of feature filters followed by a special class of mathematical transformations which represent the sensory inputs generating interacting wave fronts over the entire sensory cortical area. This transformations are now popularly known as holographic processes."[5]

This model, which is called by the name of 'Hallographic Model' seems to fulfill all sorts of essential necessities of perception. This model consolidates and retrieves the memory.[6]

For consolidation and retrieval of data, channelised from the sensory end of the apparatus holographic model requires an adjacent source which illuminates the data already available in the substratum. As long as a person is alive so long the informations coming all the while from the sensory end remain in the brain. These are unlimited in number. The locus of the informative data should always be illuminated. Due to the occurence of the memory retrieval and experience, in dream-state too, this illuminating factor should also function properly. Therefore, we have to postulate such a source which is present all the while in every human being which illuminates, observes and retrieves all sensory data, in the absence of this source not a single vital function namely, mentation, ideation etc. will ever take place. We may designate this exclusively necessary source as 'Super Consciousness' (S.C.)[7]

In dream-state this source has to be executed. In this state data is already available in the brain. Sometimes the S.C. revokes the data in very simple way sometimes it adopts a choatic fashion. This S.C. is present all through in our life. In dreamless sleep also S.C. being present cannot function because of its dissociation from the sensory cortex of the brain. Because of the presence of S.C. after getting up from this state person is capable to recall his experience of bliss.[8]

Modern Scientists have equated 'Self' as S.C. It is absolutely necessary to finger out that "From the modern theory of holographic principles used in modelling sensory and perceptual processes, the presence of super consciousness is a physical necessity. Without Super Consciousness even normal perceptual processes cannot take place."[9]

NOTES AND REFERENCES

1. Subramanyam, H.S. "Physiology And Psychology Of Perception", Sense Perception in Science & Śāstras pp. 70-71.
2. Ibid, p. 73
3. Ibid, p. 79.
4. Ibid, pp. 80-81.
5. Srinivasan, T.M. "Consciousness In Perception", *Sense Perception In Science And Śāstras, pp. 102-3.*
6. *Ibid, pp. 105.*
7. *Ibid, p. 106.*
8. *Ibid, p. 108.*
9. *Ibid, p. 109.*

V.1.1. EPISTEMOLOGY OF DREAM PERCEPTION FROM THE POINT OF VIEW OF MODERN PSYCHOLOGISTS.

At the very outset, while describing the process of dream Freud says "From the moment when we seek to penetrate more deeply into the psychic process in dreaming, all paths lead into darkness". Because we do not have proper psychological knowledge by which we can trace out a definite explanation. We may simply draw some inferences on the basis of some psychological investigation of dreams. On the other hand, under compulsion we have to go on making unlimited number of new assumptions. Of course, this will work a bit more than anticipated. Without going beyond this, we have to be dependent upon simplest logical construction.[1]

According to Freud dream is significant free psychic phenomenon. This phenomenon is motivated by a constant wish-craved fullfilment. Of course, sometimes we cannot realise its motive because of the operation of the censorship, since during the formation of dream it is subjected to censorship. In course of dream-formation beside the need of escaping the censorship some factors are also involved in its formation namely, out of necessity psychic materials condense themselves, sensory images are to be regarded for their representability and lastly the importance towards the explicit and retional external structure of dream.[2]

Freud has tried to establish a definite sequence between the psychic apparatus and the dream-formation. According to him the psychic apparatus is an assembled instrument. Each componant part of this instrument has been designated by either of these two terms 'instances' or 'systems'. This apparatus has a proper direction. Being provoked either by inner or outer stimuli our psychic activities proceed from sensory end to motor end. Sensory-end always receives perceptive stimulus and the motor end remove the sluices of motion.

The common characteristic of this psychic process is that it runs from the perceptive end to the motor end. If we put all these concepts in a diagram then the appearance of that linear diagram will be as follows:

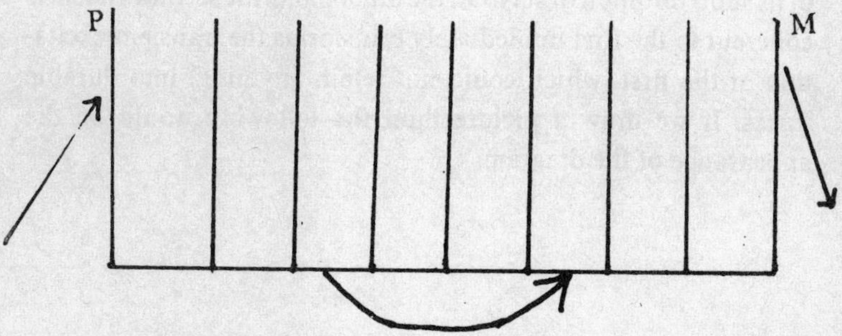

Fig. 1

But it operates only in accordance with the basic requirement. It never satisfies requirements fully. Because, this system doesnot retain the reflected act of psychic process. So this is partially fulfilled.[3]

So under compulsion Freud has drawn another picture, taking into account the loopholes of the first diagram. The speciality of this diagram is it preserves the reflex traces created by the every psychic act. The perceptive end supplies whatever stimulus goes away after producing some sort of trace in the psychic apparatus, which we may designate otherwise as memory-trace. 'The memory' is the name of the function related to these memory-traces. Freud says, if we want to co-relate the psychic process into systems, then we have to think about memory-traces as are made up by durable changes in the constituent elements of the systems. But this is quite impossible. If at all we accept, we have to agree upon two types of functioning by one and the same apparatus. It is obviously difficult to reserve changes in its elements and again to receive fresh incidence of change. Because at a time one cannot play double role. As a matter of fact, we have to assign these two functions to two different systems. Otherwise the adopted method by Freud remains unintelligible.

Freud held this view that an initial system first of all act as a receiver of outward perceptive stimulus but preserves nothing out of them. So that stimuli could not produce memory-trace because of its short duration of stay. On the other hand, the second system is coherent to the first immediately transforms the transient excitation of the first (which could not retain anything) into durable traces. If we draw a picture than the following would be the appearance of the diagram.

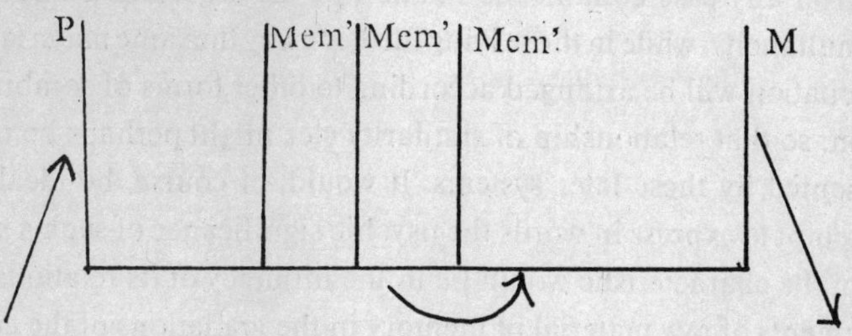

Fig. 2

The object of perception acts upon the perceptive end of the apparatus which we call symbolically P-system which not only retains the content but also retains something more than that content permanently. It is also proved that the objects of perception are connected with each other in the memory and this happens especially when the percepts occurred simultaneously. In other term this is called 'the fact of association'. If the p-system lacks in memory then it won't be capable to retain memory traces for the associations. Because, each distinct P-element will inhibit in the action if a remainder of an earlier connection exercises its power against a new perception. Therefore, we have to posit that memory system is the base of the association. Now, the fact of association will function for reducing the resistance and make the path smoother in between the mem-elements. And as a result of it excitation transmits from first to second mem-element and never to third one.

Further investigation, carried out by Freud shows clearly that "It is necessary to assume not one but many such mem-systems, in which the same excitation transmitted by the P-elements undergoes a diversified fixation. The first of these mem-systems will in any case contain the fixation of the association through simultaneity, while in those lying further away the same material of excitation will be arranged according to other forms of combination; so that relationship of similarity etc., might perhaps be represented by these later systems. It would, of course, be ideal to attempt to express in words the psychic significance of such a system. Its characteristic would lie in the intimacy of its relations to elements of raw material of memory in the gradations of the conductive resistance on the way to these elements". The P-system has no capability to retain changes. So it has no memory. Since it has no memory, it furnishes the complexity and variety of the sensory qualities to the consciousness. On the contrary, our memories are unconscious by nature. But there is no dispute over that they reveal their all sorts of activities in the unconscious state. The very character of our memory-traces is based upon our impressions.

And that too, out of so many impressions which have affected us deeply, they remain precisely in the form of memory trace. Being conscious, memories do not show any sensory quality, if at all they show, they are very negligible in comparison to the perceptions. It can be clarified that for concisouness memory and quality, both are mutually employed in the component parts of the apparatus. By this we have acquired the most convincing notion about the determination of the neuron excitations.

Freud says that "The composition of the psychic apparatus at the sensible end has been assumed regardless of dreams and of the psychological explanations which we have hitherto derived from them." But dreams play an important role in order to corroborate the fact that some sort of knowledge occurs at the other part of the apparatus. Unless we posit two types of psychic component parts of the apparatus. We may not venture to explain the dream-formation. Out of these two psychic component parts of the apparatus, one is subjected to activities and the other one is for criticism. And for this reason only consciousness will be excluded. The criticising 'instance' keeps close association with consciousness in comparison to the 'instance', which is criticized. It operates remaining as a screen in between the consciousness and the criticized instance. Again in another way we can identify the criticizing instance because, our waking life gets directed by this and defines our voluntary conscious activities. According to our assumption if we replace 'Instances' by 'systems', then the criticizing system will run to the motor end. Now, we shall put together both the systems in a diagram in order to get their relation confirmed to the consciousness.

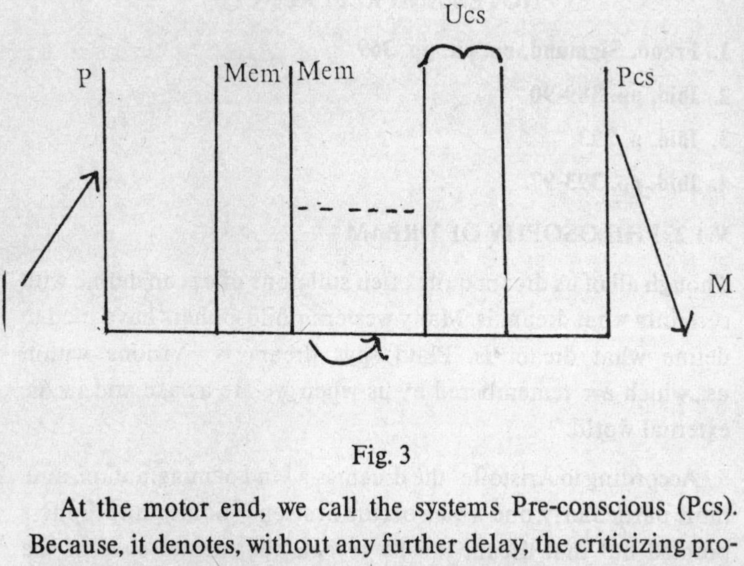

Fig. 3

At the motor end, we call the systems Pre-conscious (Pcs). Because, it denotes, without any further delay, the criticizing process in the system, which can reach to consciousness. Of course, for this, certain stipulations are to be fulfilled viz. it has to obtain a determinate degree of intensity, a certain division of that function, which is otherwise called attention. At the same time this system plays key-role of voluntary motion. At the back but quite adjacent to this Pes-system lies another system, called 'Unconcscious' (Ucs). It has no entrance to consciousness, except through the preconscious. The excitation process undergoes certain changes in the passage, through which it passes.

Now, question arises where do we localize the impulses to dream-formation. If we say that we localize it in the Ucs system it is not correct. Because, dream-formation is bound to keep communication with dream-thoughts, which are the inhabitant of Pcs-System. Moreover, we say the unconscious system is the beginning point for dream-formation. Because, the impelling energy is built up by the Unconscious. Alike all other thought structure dream-excitation struggles hard in the Pcs-system to get admitted in the conscious state.[4] This is in short what the modern psychologists say about the epistemology of dream perception.

NOTES AND REFERENCES

1. **Freud, Sigmund, op. cit, pp. 369**
2. **Ibid, pp. 389-90**
3. **Ibid, p. 393.**
4. **Ibid, pp. 393-97.**

V.1.2. PHILOSOPHY OF DREAM

Though all of us dream quite often still none of us can define with certainty what dream is. Many western philosophers have tried to define what dream is. Plato says dream is "Visions within us...which are remembered by us when we are awake and in the external world."[1]

According to Aristotle "the dream is a kind of imagination, and, more particularly, one which occurs in sleep."[2] Some philosophers pointed out that dream mostly reveals the mental state of the dreamer. But before the Freud's doctrine of sub-conscious state of mind none tried with proper care to study the dream by this way. Freud had very little to say about the nature of dream. The contention among the western philosophers is mainly based upon this issue.[3] We experience dream as real as our day-to-day experience. First of all, William James stated in his book entitled 'Principles of Psychology', "The world of dreams is our real world whilst we are sleeping, because our attention then lapses from the sensible world. Conversely, when we wake the attention usually lapses from the dream-world and that becomes unreal".[4] Having known the analogy of both states namely, the awakened-state and the dream-state Philosophers have advanced a couple of questions. Plato asks "How can you prove whether at this moment we are sleeping, and all our thoughts are a dream; or whether we are awake, and talking to one another in the waking state."[5]

In order to differentiate dream from reality Descartes put-forth his 'method of universal doubt'. He says: "I see so manifestly that there are no certain indications by which we may clearly distinguish wakefulness from sleep that I am lost in astonishment.[6] Finally, he established a criterion of consistency. He says that "For at present I find a very notable difference between the two, in as much as our memory can never connect over dreams with one another, or with the whole course of our lives, as it unites events which happen to us while we are awake."[7]

This theory was followed by several philosophers belonging to the present time. But this criterion doesnot fulfil the expected requirement. Because, 'consistency' is a term which can be employed to get tested a definite experience with regard to its future happenings.[8]

If we apply this particular term then it will facilitate a person to speak out that "I had been dreaming" and not "I am dreaming now". However highly confident about the reality of the surroundings, a person, in near future something may happen which will reveal all those reality as a part of his dream. Again, the difficulty arises whether any sort of consistency discovered is real or unreal like dream? So this word does not stand in test. Memory gives rise to genuine doubt. It may be corroborated by this sentence that 'I am not sure whether this particular event has occurred in dream or not'. When such is the case we try to remember some part of the happenings which has left stress in our memory. And if it is not possible on our part we simply sum up 'I had dreamt'. Descartes passed a remark that 'it is rare that we are in doubt about whether we are dreaming". On the other hand, the expression like 'I must be dreaming' obviously indicates that 'I am not dreaming' and this type of expression takes place when we convey astonishment of a pleasant event e.g. the arrival of a friend who was thought of to be far away. Sometimes in dream we become aware that "We are dreaming." Generally dream is real. Question doesnot arise about its genuineness. And dream is not caused by earlier doubt. In some cases dream convinces us about its reality and it never gives rise to doubt during its course.

Dream is different from hallucination and that distinction lies in the fact. There is no such external entity with whom an event of dream can be compared minutely. Because, while examining they never show 1:1 similarity with external reality. Many Philosophers have sought to examine its real aspect by using some marks. But as a matter of fact, any symbol of reality can be copied in dream. The duplicity of an entity makes it unreal. And if all dreams carry that type of symbol, which is unreal then there will be no confusion in their remembrance.

It is widely accepted that dreams are caused by the imagination and not by the intellect or senses. Here, someone claims that the word 'imagination' has been used vaguely. It does not solve the problem, rather, it puts the reader in perplexed position.[9]

Some recent Physiological work has laid down their opinion by saying that the phenomenon of dreaming and rapid-eye-movements, both are co-related.[10] This opinion of the Psychologists support the view of Aristotle i.e. "dreaming is an activity of the sensitive faculty, but of it as being imaginative."[11] But this physiological criterion of dream has been refuted by Norman Malcolm in his book 'Dreaming.'[12] This author has taken into account all earlier opinions of the philosophers. Of course, his main aim was to refute the stand of the philosophers like Descartes and Russell. Because, they arrived at a conclusion that "Our waking experiences are not intrinsically distinguishable from the delusive experiences that make up our dreams." On the contrary,

Prof. Malcolm says "dreams are not delusive experiences, because they are not experiences at all."[13]

He further asserts that "Waking testimony is the sole criterion of dreaming."[14] Prof. Malcolm nullified some general belief namely, that external stimuli cause dream; a violent dream-vision can be known from the bodily movement of a sleeper etc. by determining the 'sound-sleep' exclusively is proper time for the occurrence of dream.[15]

Not only he asserts about the occurrence of dream in sound-sleep but he also says that a person who is in sound-sleep-state will never be in a position to respond to the external stimuli.[16] Someone may say that Malcolm has critisized the Physiologists to achieve his purpose by introducing a new concept of dreaming. Because, the common notion includes with certainty the possibility of dreaming in ordinary sleep and sometimes a dreamer becomes aware that he is dreaming. To rule out both notions he forwarded a philosophical argumentative view, though it was critisized by A.J. Ayer at the later stage.[17]

But Malcolm's observation is so minute and powerful that a critic like A.J. Ayer found that it is not an easy job to refute his sayings. The reasonings advanced by Prof. Malcolm are purely based upon the 'Philosophical Investigation' of Wittgenstein. Wittgenstein holds the view that "an inner process stands in need of outward criteria."[18] Malcolm further argues that we can get the proper concept of dreaming if we give much importance to the description of dream i.e. "from the familiar phenomenon that we call 'telling a dream'." [19]

He says that in a sentence when we use 'I remember a dream' there the use of the word 'remember' is in the sense of other than normal. There is no such external criterion by which we can examine our memory. But to remember something is a special function of mind by which we go back to the past memory. And this can be examined by ourselves. We have to rely upon the statement of the dreamer, because, there is no alternative way to search out what has happened inside the dreamer during his sleep unless and until he tells sincerely.[20]

Of course, among Psychologists Freud paid much importance to the statement of the dreamer on the basis of which he tried to assess the validity of the dreamt-event.[21]

Ayer suggested to Malcolm that his theory implies that "we do not dream but only wake with delusive memories of experiences we have never had."[22] Malcolm rejects the suggestion of Ayer. Because, he is correct in stressing the significance of the report of the dreamer and the distinction of such report with the report of our public world. According to him Whatever a dreamer says after coming back to the awakened-state is final. By the word 'dream' Malcolm wants to mean that it does not prohibit its further employment of being extended by other experience, e.g. the mutual relationship between the dream report and the observation of the dreamer totally called dream.[23]

If Prof. Malcolm wants to maintain that words are to be used after proper verification of application then a host of ordinary usages would be discarded.

For the time being we accepted that the concept of dream is some sort of mental activity. But this notion is subject to be modified further in course of time, e.g. scientists uses tentatively many such concepts which convey the approximate meaning but in course of time i.e. after the completion of investigation they get confirmed what that particular term means. Malcolm claims that his employed words exclusively refer the 'inner process' and the primary meaning of the word 'dreaming' confidently refers to the report of dream but certainly it cannot inhibit its over application, which is not intended.[24]

It is quite impossible on the part of a sleeper who is asleep to be aware of anything. Many may claim that in course of sleep they became aware that they were dreaming. This type of statement signifies that they were aware that they were asleep.[25] As a matter of fact, one has to be awakened partially in sleep, when dream takes place. At the end Malcolm conluded that dream is a pseudo-problem. According to him dream is not at all an experience. It may be illusion or imagination.[26] On the other hand, Ayer concluded that dreams are purely experiences but most of them are illusions. Because, the criterion used for illusion can be applied to dream as well. Ayer doesnot think Malcolm's emphasization on the report of dream as correct. And it is also not proper to term dream-knowledge as illusion. Because, during dream there is no chance of assertion about one's experiences by others. So this knowledge can no longer be designated as illusion. It is very much difficult to reject dream as an experience. Though it appears as vague for the insufficient description, which is incapable to cover up mental phenomenon like dream. It may also be claimed that if the 'talking of dreams' are fabricated by images then dream will be considered as an example of mental imagery, which is a vague concept.[27] Despite of Malcolm's work on dream the problem of the nature of dream is still open for philosophical discussion.[28]

NOTES AND REFERENCES

1. *Jowett, B. (Tr.) The Dialougues of Plato,* p. 26.
2. Mckeon, Richard (ed), *The Basic works of Aristotle, p.625*
3. Manser, A.R. :"Dreams" *The Encyclopedia of Philosophy,* p. 414.
4. James, William, *Principles of Psychology,* p. 294
5. *The Dialougues of Plato,* op. cit. (158A, Theaetetus) p. 160.
6. Descartes, Rene, "Meditationes de Prima Philosophia", p. 146.
7. Ibid, p. 199.
8. *The Encyclopedia of Philosophy,* op. cit. p. 415
9. Ibid
10. Dement, W., and Kleitman, N, op. cit. p. 339-46.

11. *The Basic Works of Aristotle*, op. cit., p.
12. Malcolm, Narman, *Dreaming, p. 81.*
13. Ayer, A.J., *"Professor Malcolm on Dreams"* p. 517.
14. *Dreaming*, op. cit. p. 81.
15. *Dreaming*,op. cit. pp. 25-26
16. Ibid, pp. 25-26
17. "Professor Malcolm on Dreams", op. cit.pp. 517-'35.
18. Wittgenstein, L., *Philosophical Investigations*, pp. 184, 222-23.
19. *Dreaming*, op. cit. p. 55.
20. *Dreaming*, op. cit., pp. 56-58.
21. Freud, Sigmund, *The Interpretation of Dreams*,
22. "Professor Malcolm On Dreams", op. cit. p. 525
23. *The Encyclopedia of Philosophy*, op. cit. pp. 416.
24. Manser, A.R., "Dreams" Op. cit., pp. 416
25. *Dreaming*, op. cit.p 66.
26. *Dreaming*, op. cit.
27. "Professor Malcolm on Dreams", op. cit., pp. 517-'35
28. "Dreams", op. cit., p. 417

CHAPTER-VI

COMPARISON & CONCLUSION

VI.0. COMPARISON AND CONCLUSION

From what we have discussed so far the following conclusions can be drawn: Western Psychologists do not favour the ancient theories, because, according to them, ancient theories are based on hypotheses. Whereas modern theories regarding sleep and dream are the results of experiments in a laboratory.

Western Psychologists say that dream is a free psychic phenomenon which occurs during sleep. They claim that dreaming in sleep is a basic human pattern and it may occur at any time. This notion we do not find in Indian tradition. As per our division of consciousness, dream occurs particularly in the dream-state.

The Psycho-analysis of Freud unearthed the subconscious-state of mind and tried to findout the roots of mental life in the form of suppressed desire, congregated in the sub-conscious-state of mind.

In the Indian tradition too, we find that Jaina Philosophers were aware of the sub-conscious state of mind which I have already discussed in the corresponding chapter, dealing with their views. Again the broad principles of dream-vision as found in the *Bhagavati sūtra* touch upon the comprehensive theories on dream propounded by Freud, Jung, Adler etc. This is the claim of the Jaina Psychologists. In modern western Psychology sleep is of three types; (i) light sleep (ii) middle sleep and (iii) deep sleep. Generally in the first two, dream takes place. But this does not mean that in deep-sleep dream does not occur. Dream does occur in this state also but we cannot remember the dreamt-event. Normal people remember only an insignificant fraction of their total dream because of distortion. Moreover, in the first two states dream-contents are manifest but in deep-sleep, the contents are latent.

According to Indian Medical science *(Āyurveda) Vaikārikī-nidrā* alone represents both the states, *svapna*, (dream-consciousness) as well as *suṣupti* (dreamless-sleep). From Psycho-analytical point of view, sleep is divided into two types: Paradoxical-sleep and Orthodox-sleep. The Rapid-Eye-Movements (REMS) indicate the Paradoxical-sleep. And in Orthodox-sleep the contrary is the case. This sleep seems to be the state of deep-sleep.

Western Psychologists are of the opinion that dream is a regular, involuntary mental activity in sleep. They further hold the view that there is no pure dreamless sleep, nor any time mind is completely at rest. This view goes against the Indian tradition.

Non-REM sleep seems to be the blissful unity of mind, which may be equated with the Indian traditional notion of Suṣupti.

In deep-sleep-state, no knowledge is possible. Because, external stimuli cannot enter in memory in this state of sleep. Sounds or smells are perceived and evaluated, then they are discarded or being horrified by some scene, the person is awakened. To this view, no profound metaphysical truth is revealed by deep-sleep. Western Philosophers also support the same view by saying that in sound-sleep state a person cannot respond to outward stimuli. This is why perhaps, the Āyurvedins say that one has to remain awake partially in sleep and that is the proper time for any dream-knowledge.

In course of discussion one will never come across concept of dream as deity in western Psychological treatises. Because, their way of approach is altogether different than that of the Indian seers. This Vedic notion came into existence perhaps, because of the superstitious mind of the people during the Vedic era.

In the Indian tradition sometimes it is said that a dream is produced by god. But it is evident that such a view has no rationale. That is why the Indian Philosophers pointed out that the dream-experiences are nothing, the products of *vāsanā* (i.e. the impression), left behind by the awakened-state experience and *Saṁskāras.* Of course, they have not, identified *saṁskāras* of only one birth which are responsible for dream-knowledge but they can be traced to any birth in the *Jiva's journey of the saṁsāra.* Though the *saṁskāras* are the base of the dream-experiences there are not mere revival or reproduction of the past. Because, dream-experiences show inconsistency, contradiction and extra-ordinary events. We may deduce that these are caused by false *saṁskāra.* So in a way, the subjective reality of dream depends upon the objective reality. In otherwords, dreams are objective world oriented. Some western Philosophers too held the same view.[1]

As western Psycho-analysts give much importance to the stimuli, Indian Philosophers attach importance to *saṁskāras.* Moreover, a *Jiva* doesnot create the dream-vision in the strict sense of the term 'creation'. It is an automatic flow of suppressed desire. Western Psychologists also agree on this point.

Western Psychologists hold that sleep is not a required factor in the fabrication of dream from the conventional meaning point of the term 'sleep'. On the otherhand, the Indian philosopher points out that *nidrā* (i.e. the sleep) is *sahakārikārana* (auxiliary cause) of dream.

Dream represents real and unreal nature in both the traditions. In the test of reality of dream, the western tradition regards dream as an exotic, an appetizer to titillate the mind of a dreamer for a while. Whereas, in some section of the Indian Philosophical traditions it has been accepted as clue to declare the world as unreal.

Indian and western Philosophers regard dream as an illusion, it has nothing common with the intellectual complications. As long as a person dreams so long this phenomenon is true and this view is equally shared by the Philosophers of both the traditions.

In dream, a sight which was pleasing or distressing the dreamer, by the opening of the eyes goes back into nothingness. In otherwords, it proves the nothingness of the dream-universe. This might be the reason to cite the voidness dream as an example to falsify the entire universe, which is also illusory and void according to the Advaitins and Idealists.

It is interesting to note that although we have many mistaken knowledges namely, *śukti-rajatajñāna* etc. in the awakened-state itself, still, the Indian Philosophers cite example from dream-state. The simple reason behind this may be that the appearance of the world is not as false as the objects of the analogus perception like *śukti-rajata or rajju-sarpa* which are contradicted immediately. So from the point of view of falsity both the knowledges are not one and the same. Because, there is difference in the duration of their existence. The duration of *Prātibhāsikasattā* of dream-objects is longer than that of the objects of a wrong knowledge of the awakened state. The *Vyavahārikasattā* of the objects of the true knowledge of the awakened-state is also contradicted after the knowledge of the Brahman. So, it is out of necessity of Philosophical analysis they opted for one full-fledged state, which is utterly false. Further, taking into consideration the diagnostic aspect of dream as some psychologists have tried to fix up the reality of the dream. Likewise, the diagnostic value also prevailed in the vedic literature. Vedic seers used to demonstrate the way of protection, having known the bad effects of the dream-symbols. We find the same trend in some Philosophies of the later-age. That the dream-knowledge shows discrepancy with the external objects and that it has no external object are also shared by both Western and Eastern traditions. But Indian, dream-epistemology is better than that of the Western. Because, Indian Philosophers accept the presence of ā tman as sākṣin. This is why some Indian Philosophers hold that dream-knowledge is determinate one. Because, it never oscillates in between two things.[2]

Now, let us judge what sort of reality this knowledge possesses. According to those who cite dream-knowledge as an example, the reality is relative in character. The difference is only in the duration of time. And due to this reason only apart from the absolute reality (i.e. the Brahman) neither this mundane universe nor this dream-world is real. This is why the entities of the mundane universe have only *vyavahārika-sattā* and those of the dream-state have only *Prā tibhāsika-sattā (i.e. jñānaikasattā)* and the 'Brahman' alone has the *Pāramārthika-sattā*.

As regards the status of dream-object it is to be decided in the light of the definition of truth. Dream objects cannot be considered as real as those experienced in our awakened-state, nor can they be dismissed as totally fictitoius or unreal as mirage or silver-nacre. A safer way to do so is to define a true knowledge as that knowledge which is not followed by a contradictory knowledge (i.e. *bā dhakajñāna)* and a false-knowledge is that which is followed by a contradictory knowledge. Let us apply this notion of truth and falsity to the following knowledges:

(i) The knowledge of a snake after seeing the rope in the awakened-state.

(ii) The knowledge of a real snake in the awakened-state

(iii) The knowledge of a snake after seeing the rope in the dream-state, and

(iv) The knowledge of a real-snake in the dream-state.

So far the human response is concerned, in all the four cases, it is the same. But the result of the behaviour is not the same, relatively. The snake of the dream-state also bites and a person dies out of that in the dream. Similarly, the snake bites at the awakened-state and a person dies out of that. While the knowledge 'X' died of snake-bite' in the dream is followed by another knowledge which is a contradictory knowledge when he gets up from dream and finds that he is alive, there is no such knowledge which contradicts the knowledge of a person-who dies of snake-bite at the awakened-state. Therefore, in comparison to the snake of the dream-state the snake of the awakened-state is called real. Hence, both knowledges are not one and the same and therefore, the knowledge of dream cannot be treated as on par with the knowledge of the awakened state. Similarly, seeing of the snake in rope in both the states is followed by a contradictory knowledge namely, 'It is not a snake'. Hence, in comparison to the snake of that mistaken knowledge, the snake which kills a person is said to be real. Thus, a knowledge is real or its object is real till the *bādhakajñāna* arises. Thus, the snake of the erroneous knowledge was real till it was not known that it was rope. The snake of the dream which killed the person was real till one got up and found that the person is alive. The snake of the awakened-state also is likewise real till the *bādhaka-jñ*āna arises that it is not a snake. Such *bādhakajñ*āna will arise, after the Brahman is known i.e. at a still different-state in comparison to the state which we know now as the awakened-state. Again, for those who define truth to include all experiences, the dream-experiences are treated as true. But for those who define truth as constant and not sublated at any stage not only dream-experiences are false, but also awakened-state experiences are false. Some western Philosophers tried to fix up the criterion of consistency. But they couldnot succeed in doing so.[3] Among Indian Philosophers Bhasaravajñ*a correctly pointed out the criterion of a real object.*

According to him any knowledge will be declared as true provided it possesses (i) arthakriyākāritva (i.e. the consistent behaviour), (ii) *saṁvāditva* (i.e. one-to-one correspondence with the existent object and (iii) *upalabdhitva* (i.e. the real apprehension).

From all these it may be concluded that ancient Indian analysis of dream is more analytical and philosophical than physiological. On the otherhand, western analysis is more physiological than philosophical or analytical and the western psycho-analytical findings also have not produced any remarkable head-way by which we can further examine our Indian speculative analysis.

NOTES AND REFERENCES

1. *Philosophical Investigations,* op. cit. pp. 184, 222-'23.

2. *Kir.*, op. cit, pp. 180
3. Descartes, Rane. op. cit. pp. 199.

BIBLIOGRAPHY

I. Primary Sources

II. Secondary Sources

I. *Primary Sources:*

1. *Aṇubhāṣya* of Vallabhacārya. Edited with a new commentary the Bālabodhini by Pt. Shridhar Tryambak Pathak, Part II, Poona, 1926.

2. *Advayavajrasaṁgraha*, edited with an Introduction by Haraprasad Shastri, Oriental Institute, Baroda, 1927.

3. *Abhidharmakośabhāṣya* of Vasubandhu, Edited by P. Pradhan, Published by K.P. Jayaswal Research Institute, Patna, 1967.

4. *Ādipurāṇa* of Ācārya Jinasena. Edited by Pt. Pannalal Jain, Published by Bhāratiya Jñānapiṭha, Varanasi, 1965.

5. *Āyurvedīya Mahākaṣa, ed. by Venimādhava Sāstri Joshi + Nā rāyana H. Joshi, Pub. by the Maharashtra State Literature & Cultural Association*, Bombay, 1968.

6. *Ālambanaparīkṣā* of Diṅnāga with the commt. of Dharmapā la, Translated into English and restored into Skt. from Tibetan and chines versions and edited by N. Aiyaswami-śāstri, Pub. by the Adyar Library, Madras. 1942.

7. *Ṛgveda-Saṁhitā*, with the commentary of Sāyaṇācārya, Vol. II, III & IV, Published by the Vaidika Saṁśodhana Maṇḍala, Poona, 1978.

8. *Kaṇādasūtra vivṛtti* by Jayanārāyaṇa Tarkapañcānana, Calcutta, 1861.

9. *Kalpasūtra* of Bhadrabahu Svami, Trans. by K.C. Lalwani, Pub. by Motilal Banarsidas, Delhi, 1979.

10. *Kāṭhaka-Saṁkalana*. Edited with notes by Suryakānta MCLD Publications, New Delhi, 1981.

11. *Kiraṇāvali* of Udayanācārya. Edited by Jitendra S. Jetly, Published by the Oriental Institute, Baroda, 1971.

12. *Jainendra Siddhānta Kośa* of Kshu Jainendra Varṇī. Edited by Dr. Hiralal Jain and Dr. A.N. Upadhye, Published by Bhā ratiya Jñānapiṭha, Varanasi, 1973.

13. *Tattvacintāmani* of Gaṅgeśa, (Anumānakhanda) with the commt. of Dharmarajdvari & Rucidatta Mishra, Tirupati ed, 1982.

14. *Tattvasaṁgraha* of Śāntarakṣita, Part II, with the commentary Pañcikā by Kamalashila, Critically edited by Swami Dwarikadas Shastri, Published by Baudha Bharati, Varanasi, 1968.

15. *Tarkabhāṣā* of Keśava Miśra. Edited by Pt. Shri Shobhitā Miśra, Published by Chowkhamba Sanskrit Series Office, Benaras, 1953.

16. *Tarkasaṁgraha* of Annambhaṭṭa with the author's own *Dīpikā* and Govardhane's *Nyāya-Bodhini*, edited by Y.V. Athalye & M.R. Bodas. Second edition Published by Bhandarkar Oriental Research Institute. 1930.

17. *Tarkāmṛta* of Jagadīśa Tarkālaṁkāra with *vivriti* by J.K. Tarkatī rtha, Published by The Asiatic Society, 1974.

18. *Nandisuttam* of Devavācaka. Edited by Puppha Bhikkhu Published by Sūtrāgama Prakāsaka Samiti, Gurgaon, 1954.

19. *Nāmaliṅgānuśāsana or Amarakoṣa*, Edited by Pt. Hara govinda Sāstri, Chowkhamba Sanskrit Series, Varanasi, Vol. I. 1970.

20. *Nilakanṭhī on Tarkasaṁgraha dīpikā* by Nilakaṇṭha Bhaṭṭah, Benaras, 1875.

21. *Nyāyakusumāñjali* of Udayanācārya, Edited by Pt. Dhuṇḍhirā ja Śāstri, Published by Chowkhamba Sanskrit Series Office,

Varanasi, 1957.

22. *Nyāyakośa* Edited by Bhīmācārya Jhalakīkār, Revised and re-edited by V.S. Abhyankar, Bhandarkar Oriental Research Institute, Poona, 1978.
23. *Nyāyadarśanam* with vātsyāyana's *Bhāṣya*, Uddyotkara's *Vārtika*, Vācaspati Miśra's *Tātparyaṭikā* and Viśvanātha's Vṛtti, Critically edited with notes by Taranatha Nyaya Tarkatirtha and Amarendramohan Tarkatirtha, Published by Munshiram Manoharlal Publishers Pvt. Ltd., 2nd edition, Delhi,1985.
24. *Nyāyapraveśa of Diṅnāga*, part. I. with the commentaries *Nyāyapraveśavṛtti* by Haribhadrasūri and *Nyāya-praveśavṛtti-Pañcikā* by Pārśvadeva, Critically edited by Anandsankar B. Dhruva, Published by the Oriental Institute of Baroda, Baroda, 1968.
25. Ibid, Part II, edited by Vidhushekhara Bhattacharya, Published by N.M. Dutt on behalf of the Central Library of Baroda, 1927.
26. *Nyāyabindu* of Dharmakīrti with the Commentaries *Pradipa* of Dharmottarācārya and Durvekamiśra's commentary. Published by K.P. Jayaswal Research Institute, Patna; 1955.
27. *Nyāyabhūṣaṇam* of Bhāsarvajña, A commentary of Nyāyasāra, Edited by Svāmi Yogindrānandaḥ, Published by Saḍdarśana Prakāśana Pratiṣṭhānam, Varanasi, 1968.
28. *Nyāyamañjarī* of Jayantabhaṭṭa, critically edited by K.S. Varadacharya, Published by the Oriental Research Institute, Mysore, 1969.
29. *Nyāya-Līlāvati* of Vallabhāchārya, edited by Pt. Dhuṇḍhirāja Śāstri, published by the Chowkhamba Skt. Series Office, Benaras, 1933.
30. *Nyāyasāra* of Bhāsaravajña with the Commentary Nyāyamuktāvali of Aparārkadeva, edited by S. Subrahmanya Sastri, Published under the auspices of Madras Govt. Oriental Series,

Madras, 1961.

31. Ibid. with the commentary *Pañcikā* of Vāsudeva, Critically edited by V.S. Abhyankar and C.R. Devadhar, Poona, 1922.
32. *Pātañjala Yogasūtra* with the *Vṛtti* of Bhojadeva, Edited by Dr. Ramsarikar Bhaṭṭācārya, Published by Bhāratīya Vidyā Prakā śana, Varanasi, 1979.
33. *Pramāṇavārtikam* of Dharmakīrti *(Svārthānumānapari-cchedah)* with the commentary of Karṇakagobhi, Edited by Rā hula Sāṁkṛtyāyana, Kitab Mahal, Allahabad, 1943.
34. bid *(Pratyakṣakhaṇda)* with the commentary *vṛtti* of Manorathanandin, Critically edited by Svami Dwarikadas Shastri, Published by Bauddha Bharati, Varanasi, 1984.
35. *Praśastapādabhāṣya* of Praśastadeva with the commentary *Nyāyakandali* by Sridhara Bhatta, Edited by Pt. Durgādhara Jhā, Published by the Sampurnananda Sanskrit Visvavidyalaya, Varanasi, 1977.
36. *Bṛhati* of Prabhākara Miśra, Edited by S.K. Ramanatha Sastri, Published by the Madras University, Madras, 1937.
37. *Bodhicāryāvatāra* of Śāntadeva, with the commt. *Pañjikā* by Prajñākaramati, edited by Dr. P.L. Vaidya, Published by the Mithla Institute, Darbhanga, 1960.
38. *Brahma-Mimāṁsā-Bhāsya, A commentary on Brahmasūtras* called *Vedānta-Pārijāta-Saurabha* by Nimbārkācārya, Edited by Vindhyeswariprasād Dvivedin Benaras, 1967.
39. *Brahmasūtrabhāṣya* of Maddhvācārya, by Raṅgācarya Bā lkṛshnācārya Reddi, Pune, 1926.
40. *Brahmasūtrabhāṣyam* of Sri Bhāskarācārya, Edited by Pt. Vindhyesvari Prasāda Dvivedin, Chowkhamba Sanskrit Series, Benaras, 1903.
41. *Brahmasūtra-Śaṅkara-Bhāsya. with the commentaries Bhā mati, Vedantakalpataru & Kalpataruparimala* Vol. II,

Published by Parimal Publications, First Edition, Ahmedbad, 1981.

42. *Māṇḍukyopaniṣad* with Gauḍapāda's *Kārikā* and Śaṁkara's Commentary, Translated and Annotated by Swāmi Nikhilananda, Published by Sri Ramakrishna Ashrama, 1st edition, Mysore, 1936.
43. *Mādhyamakaśāstra* of Nāgārjuna with Commentary *Prasannapadā by Chandrakīrtti, Edited by Swami Dwarikadas Shastri, Published by Bauddha Bharati, Varanasi, 1983.*
44. *Mimāṁsādarśanam* of Jaimini, Re-edited by K.V. Abhyaṅkara, Published by the Anandāśrama Sanskrit Series, Poona, 1976.
45. *Viśeṣāvāśyakabhāṣyam* with Śiṣyahita *Bṛhadvṛtti* by Māladhā ri Hemachandra, Published by Shah Harakchandra Bhurabhai, Benaras, 1914.
46. *Vaidika-Padānukrama-koṣa*, Edited by Vishva Bandhu, Vol. XIII, Hoshiarpur, 1962.
47. *Vaiśesikadarśanam* of Kaṇāda with the commentary of *Upaskā ra* by Śaṅkara Miśra, Edited by Dhuṇḍhirāja Sāstri, Published by the Chowkhamba Sanskrit Series Office, Varanasi, 1923.
48. *Śāstradīpikā* of Pārtha Sarathi Miśra, Edited by Dr. Kiśordas Svāmi, Published by Sri Sādhubela Saṁskṛta-mahāvidyālaya, Varanasi, 1977.
49. *Śrībhāṣya* of Rāmānuja. Edited by R.D. Karmarkar, Part III, Poona, 1964.
50. *Ślokavārtika* of Kumārila Bhaṭṭa, Edited by Svāmi Dvārikādā sa Śāstri, Published by the Tara Publications, Varanasi, 1978.
51. *Saptapadārthī* of Sivāditya, edited by D. Gurumurti, Published by Theosophical Publishing House, Adyar, Madras. 1932.

52. *Sarvadarśana-Saṁgraha* of Sāyaṇa Mādhava Edited with an original commentary in Sanskrit by Vasudev Shastri Abhyankar, Published by the Bhandarkar Oriental Research Institute, Poona, 1978.
53. *Sarvamatasaṁgraha*. edited by T. Gaṇapati Śāstrī, Trivandrum Skt. series, Trivandrum, 1918.
54. *Sāṁkhyakārikā* of Iśvarakṛṣṇa with the commentaries called *Tattvarpabhā* of Rāmaśaṁkara Tripāthī and the *Yuktidīpikā*, Edited by Rāmaśaṁkara Tripāthī, Published by Bālakṛṣṇa Tripāthī, Varanasi, 1970.
55. Ibid with the *Maṭharavṛtti of Māṭharācārya*, Edited by Pt. Vishnuprasād Śarmā and the *Jayamaṅgalā* of Śaṅkara, Critically edited by Satkariśarmā Vaṅgiya, Published by the Chowkhamba Sanskrit Series Office, Varanasi, 1970.
56. *Sāṁkhya-Yogakośa*, Edited by Kedārnāth Tripāthī, Published by Vīrendranāth Tripāthi, Varanasi, 1974.
57. *Sāmkhyasūtram* with the Commentary called *Pravacanabhāṣya* by Vijñānabhikṣu, Edited by Rāmasaṁkara Bhattacharya, Published by Bhāratīya Vidyā Prakāśana, Benaras, 1977.
58. *Sāṁgayogadarśana* with the scholium of Vyāsa and the commentaries of *Tattvavaiśāradi*, *Patañjali* Rahasya, Yoga-Vārtika and Bhāsvatī, Published by Chowkhamba Sanskrit Series Office, Benaras, 1935.
59. *Siddhāntacandrodaya* of Srikrisnadhūrjaṭidīkṣit, Venaras, 1942.
60. Syādvādamañjari of Malliṣeṇa. Edited by A.B. Dhruva, Published by Bhandarkar Oriental Research Institute, Poona, 1933.

II. *Secondary Sources:*

1. *Adler, Gerhard, Studies in Analytical Psychology*, Published by the Routledge & Kegan Paul Ltd, England, 1948.

2. *Ayer,* A.J. "Professor Malcolm on Dreams", *The Journal of Philosophy,* Vol. 57, New York, 1960.
3. *Benton, William, The Encyclopedia Britannica,* Vol. 7. Published by Encyclopedia Britannica Ltd. London, 1964.
4. *Bhavasar, S.N., Etymology in the Brāhmaṇas,* A Ph.D. Thesis submitted to the University of Poona, under the guidance of C.G. Devasthali, Pune 1969.
5. *Buck, Carl Darling, A Dictionary of Selected Synonyms in the Principal Indo-European Languages,* Chicago. 1949.
6. *Chatterji.* D.C. "The Problem of knowledge and the four school of Later Buddhism", ABORI, Poona, Vol. XII, Part 3, 1931.
7. *Colebrooke, Henry Thomas, (Tr.) Sāṁkhyakārikā* of Īśvarakrishna and Wilson, Horace Hayman (Tr.) Bhāṣya of Gauḍapāda on *Sāṁkhyakārikās,* Pub. by Tookaram Tatya, Bombay, 1887.
8. *Date, V.H. (Tr.). Vedanta Explained,* Saṁkara's commt on Brahmasūtras, Vol. 2, Published by Munshiram Manoharlal, 2nd edition, Delhi, 1973.
9. *Dement,* William and Kleitman, Nathaniel "The Relation of Eye-movements During sleep to Dream Activity", *The Journal of Experimental Psychology,. Vol. 53. No.5, 1957.*
10. *Deśćartes,* Rene, "Meditationes De Prima Philosophia" Trans. by E.S. Haldane and G.R.T. Ross in *The Philosophical Works of Descartes,* Dover Publications, Vol. I, England, 1955.
11. *Fort,* Andrew O, "Dreaming in Advaita Vedānta", *Philosophy East and West* Vol. XXXV, no. 4, U.S.A. 1985.
12. *Freud, Sigmund. The Interpretations of Dreams,* Translated by Dr. A.A. Brill, Pub. by the Modern Library, New York, 1931.
13. *Ghatage, A.M. (ed), An Encyclopedic Dictionary of Sanskrit on Historical Principles,* Vol. I, Pune, 1976.

14. *James, William, Principles of Psychology,* Vol. 2, Dover Publications, New York, 1950.

15. *Jhā, Gaṅgānāth. (Tr.) The Nyāyasūtras* of Gautama with the Bhāṣya of Vātsyāyana and Vārtika of Uddyotakara with notes from Vācaspati Miśra's Nyāya-vārtika-tātparyaṭīkā, Udayana's Pariśuddhi and Raghuṭṭama's Bhāsyachandra, Pub. by Motilal Banarsidas, Delhi, 1984.

16. *Jhā, Gaṅgānāth, The Prābhākara School of Pūrva-mīmāṁsā* Pub. by Motilal Banarsidass, Allahabad. First edition 1911.

17. *Jhā Gaṅgānāth, (Tra), The Yoga-Darśana of Patanjali with the Bhāṣya of Vyāsa and notes from vācaspati Miśra's Tattvavaiśā radī Vijñānabhikṣu's* Yogavārtika and Bhoja's Rājamārtaṇda, Pub. by Bombay Theosophical publication, Bombay, 1907.

18. Ibid. *Śābarabhāṣya*, Vol. I, published by the Oriental Institute, Baroda, 2nd edition, 1973.

19. Ibid. Ślokavārtika of Kumārila with the commentaries Kāsika and Nyāyaratnākar, Published by Sri Satguru Publications, Delhi, 1983.

20. *Jowett, B. (Tr.) The Dialogues of Plato* Published by Random House, New York, Vol. 2. (46A Timaeus), 1937.

21. *Jung, C.G., Modern Man In Search of A Soul,* Published by Kegan Paul and Co. Ltd. London, 1936.

22. *Jung. C.G. Analytical Psychology,* Pub. by Routledge & Kegan Paul Ltd. London, 1968.

23. Kalghati, T.G. "Dreams In Jain Psychology", *Proceedings of Indian Philosophical Congress, 1967.*

24. *Keith, A.B. Śāṅkhyāyana Āraṇyaka,* Pub. by the Royal Asiatic Society, London, 1908.

25. *Lalwani, K.C. (Tr.) Kalpasūtra* of Bhadrabāhu Svāmi, Published by Motilal Banarsidass, Delhi, 1979.

26. *Little, William. The Shorter Oxford English Dictionry,* on

Historical Principles Vol. I. Published by the Oxford University Press, London, Third Edition, 1944.

27. *Malcolm, Norman. Dreaming.* Published by the Routledge and Kegan Paul Ltd. London, 1959.
28. *Manser. A.R. "Dreams", The Encyclopedia of Philosophy,* edt. by Paul Edward, Vol.2, New York, 1967.
29. *Mckeon, Richard (ed), The Basic Works of Aristotle,* Pub. by Random House, New York, 1941.
30. *Mehta, Mohanlal, Outlines of Jaina Philosophy,* Published by the Jaina Mission Society, Bangalore city, 1954.
31. *Mishra, Umesh, "Dream theory in Indian thought", Allahabad University Studies,* vol. 5. 1929.
32. *O'Flaherty, W.D. Dreams, Illusion and Other Realities* Pub. by Motilal Banarsidass, Delhi, 1987.
33. *Oswald, Iwan. Sleep,* First Published by Penguin Books Ltd, Harmondsworth (England). 1966.
34. *Pandurangi, K.T.* "A Note on the Analysis of Dream-experiences in Vedānta-sūtras (3.2.1-6)", *Proceedings of the all-India Oriental Conference,* 28th session. Pub. by the Bhandarkar Oriental Research Institute, Poona, 1978.
35. *Pooter, Karl, H. The Encyclopedia of Indian Philosophies,* Vol. I, III, & IV, Published by Motilal Banarasidass, First Indian Edition, Delhi, 1981.
36. *Radhakrishnan, S, Indian Philosophy,,* Vol. I, Published by the Macmillan Company, New York, 1929.
37. *Sharma, R.R. "Yogācāra* Theory of External World", *Proceeding of the 5th AIOC.* Vol. II. (Lahore, Uni. Punjab), 1930.
38. *Shastri,* D.N. "Sautrāntika Theory of External Knowledge", ABORI, Vol. XXXII, Poona, 1952.
39. *Sikder, J.C. Studies in the Bhagawatisūtra,* Pub. by the

Research Institute of Prakrit, Jainology and Ahimsa, Varanasi, 1964.

40. *Sing, Fatah. The Vedic Etymology* Pub. by the Samskrit Sadan, 1952
41. *Sinhā*, Jadunāth, Indian Psychology: Cognition, Published by Sinha Publishing House, 2nd edition, Vol.1. 1958.
42. *Siṇhā,Nandalal (Tr.), Vaiśeṣika Sūtras* of Kaṇāda with the commt. of Saṅkara Miśra and extracts from the gloss of Jayanā rāyaṇa, Pub. by S.N. Publications. Delhi. 1986.
43. *Srinivasan, T.M, Sense Perception In Science and Śāstras,* Proceedings of the Seminar held at Bangalore, 1985.
44. *Stcherbatsky, Th., The Central Conception of Buddhism,* Published by the Royal Asiatic Society, London, 1923.
45. *Swain, B.K. Philosophy of the Mahopaniṣad,* A Dissertation submitted to the uni of Poona under the guidance of Dr. Shiv-kumar, 1985.
46. *Tripathy, C.L.* "The Problem of Knowledge in Yogācārya Buddhism", *Bharat Bharti,* Varanasi, 1972.
47. *Upadhyāya. Baladeva, Bhāratīya Darśana,* Published by Sā radā Mandir, Varanasi, 1971.
48. *Way, Lewis, Alfred Adler, An Introduction to his Psychology,* Published by the Penguin Books Ltd. Harmondsworth (England) First Published in the year 1956.
49. *Wittgenstein, L.* Philosophical Investigations Trans by E.M. Anscombe, Published by Basil Blackwell, Oxford & New York, 1953.
50. *Woodworth, Robert S. Psychology,* Published by Metuen & Co. Ltd, London, First Published in the year 1922.